ESSENTIALLY

SPEAKING

ESSENTIALLY

SPEAKING

Feminism,
Nature
&
Difference

DIANA FUSS

ROUTLEDGE
New York   London

Published in 1989 by

Routledge
An imprint of Routledge, Chapman and Hall, Inc.
29 West 35 Street
New York, NY 10001

Published in Great Britain in 1990 by

Routledge
11 New Fetter Lane
London EC4P 4EE

Library of Congress Cataloging in Publication Data

Fuss, Diana, 1960–
  Essentially speaking.

  Bibliography: p.
  Includes index.
  1. Feminism—Philosophy.   2. Essence (Philosophy)
3. Constructivism (Philosophy) I. Title.
HQ1154.F88 1989   305.42'01   89-10279
ISBN 0-415-90132-4
ISBN 0-415-90133-2 (pbk.)

British Library Cataloguing in Publication Data
Fuss, Diana, 1960–
  Essentially speaking.
  1. Feminism
  I. Title
  305.4'2

  ISBN 0-415-90132-4
  ISBN 0-415-90133-2 (pbk.)

For My Family

Contents

Acknowledgments

My first acknowledgment must certainly go to those who generously took the time to read this manuscript while it was still in its formative stages; I owe my greatest debt of thanks to Mary Ann Doane, Ellen Rooney, Robert Scholes, Naomi Schor, and Houston A. Baker, Jr. The Pembroke Center for Teaching and Research on Women at Brown University provided an exciting community of feminist scholars who energized and supported my work; I would particularly like to thank all the participants in the 1987–88 seminar who, individually and collectively, helped me to define and to articulate so many of the ideas which ultimately found their way into this book. Special thanks to Elizabeth Weed, Barbara Babcock, and Ann Fausto-Sterling. For their intellectual and emotional support, warmest thanks to Carole-Anne Tyler, Kathryn Stockton, Bill Martin, John Murchek, Evelyn Roberts, and Karen Bock.

Introduction

Has essentialism received a bad rap? Few others words in the vocabulary of contemporary critical theory are so persistently maligned, so little interrogated, and so predictably summoned as a term of infallible critique. The sheer rhetorical power of essentialism as an expression of disapprobation and disparagement was recently dramatized for me in the classroom when one of my most theoretically sophisticated students, with all the weight of recent feminist theory behind her, sought to persuade me that the Marxist-feminist text I had assigned did not deserve our serious consideration. The book, my student insisted, was "obviously essentialist" and therefore dangerously reactionary; though impassioned in its politics, the argument went, the text was nonetheless backward in its critical thinking. My response to this student's charge might also serve as the keynote to this book: in and of itself, essentialism is neither good nor bad, progressive nor reactionary, beneficial nor dangerous. The question we should be asking is not "is this text essentialist (and therefore 'bad')?" but rather, "if this text is essentialist, *what motivates its deployment?*" How does the sign "essence" circulate in various contemporary critical debates? Where, how, and why is it invoked? What are its political and textual effects? These, to me, pose the more interesting and ultimately the more difficult questions.

Essentialism is most commonly understood as a belief in the real, true essence of things, the invariable and fixed properties which define the "whatness" of a given entity. In feminist theory, the idea that men and women, for example, are identified as such on the basis of transhistorical, eternal, immutable essences has been unequivocally rejected by many anti-essentialist poststructuralist feminists concerned with resisting any attempts to naturalize human nature. And yet one can also hear echoing from the corners of the debates on essentialism renewed interest in its possibilities and potential usages, sounds which articulate themselves most often in the form of calls to "risk" or to "dare" essentialism.[1] To some, the essentialist/anti-essentialist debate marks a dangerous impasse in recent feminist theory; to others, it signifies the very condition and possibility of our theorizing.[2] To some, essentialism is nothing more than the philosophical enforcer of a liberal humanist idealism which seeks to locate and to contain the subject within a fixed set of differences. "This disease of thinking in essences," Roland Barthes charges, "is at the bottom of every bourgeois mythology of man" (1957, 75). To others, essentialism may not be without a certain tactical or interventionary value, especially in our political struggles and debates. Thus Paul Smith places essentialism within a "discourse of resistance" (1988, chapter 9) and Steven Epstein identifies essentialism as a "legitimation strategy" (1987, 20). My own view is that essentialism can be deployed effectively in the service of both idealist and materialist, progressive and reactionary, mythologizing and resistive discourses. The point of this book then is not to seek out, expose, and ultimately discredit closet essentialists but rather to investigate what purpose or function essentialism might play in a particular set of discourses.

Importantly, essentialism is typically defined in opposition to difference; the doctrine of essence is viewed as precisely that which seeks to deny or to annul the very radicality of difference. The opposition is a helpful one in that it reminds us that a complex system of cultural, social, psychical, and historical differences, and not a set of pre-existent human essences, position and constitute the subject. However, the binary articulation of essentialism and difference can also be restrictive, even obfuscating, in that it allows us to ignore or to deny the differences *within* essentialism. This book will make the claim that there is no essence to essentialism, that (historically, philosophically, and politically) we can only speak of *essentialisms*. Correlatively, it will also make the claim that constructionism (the position that differences are constructed, not innate) really operates as a more sophisticated form of essentialism. The bar between essentialism and constructionism is by no means as solid and unassailable as advocates of both sides assume it to be.

Chapter One begins the project of rethinking the essentialist/constructionist opposition by laying out the terms of the debate and demonstrating how essentialism and constructionism are deeply and inextricably co-implicated with each other. This opening chapter focuses specifically upon the work of Jacques Lacan and Jacques Derrida (two poststructuralists who have made especially important contributions to constructionist thought) in order to demonstrate how constructionism is fundamentally dependent upon essentialism in order to do its work. The second chapter considers whether social constructionists can entirely dispense with the notion of essence, and, through a close reading of the recent disputes over "reading as woman," it continues to explore the complicated relations between essentialism, deconstruction, and feminism. Chapters Three and Four further map out the terms of the essentialist/constructionist tension in feminist theory by implicitly staging a confrontation between Monique Wittig, an anti-essentialist materialist, and Luce Irigaray, an essentialist psychoanalytic philosopher. While the Wittig chapter reassesses the presumed political radicality of the social constructionist position, the Irigaray chapter re-evaluates the presumed theoretical conservatism of essentialism; each chapter attempts to refigure and, in effect, to compensate for the prevalent poststructuralist understanding of the essentialist/constructionist polemic.

Each of the remaining chapters focuses upon a current debate in which essence operates as a privileged signifier. Although clearly the issues I have targeted for discussion in the latter half of the book (race, homosexuality, pedagogy) are not discontinuous or isolated subjects, the debates which have arisen around these issues suggest that essence does not circulate through them in the same way and that its effects are often quite different. This is due less, perhaps, to any essential differences between categories and more to the important historical differences which produced and continue to shape them; because these debates do not always share the same political agendas and only infrequently cast their theoretical concerns about essentialism in the exact same terms, I have elected to discuss each topic in a separate chapter. Chapter Five, then, addresses the recent disputes amongst Afro-Americanists over the deconstruction of "race" as an essential, natural, empirical category and over the implications of this erasure of "race" for Afro-American literary criticism. Chapter Six confronts the controversy in gay and lesbian theory over both the constructionist hypothesis of an invented homosexuality and the essentialist practice of an identity politics. Finally, the conclusion attempts to bring all these related questions together in a brief examination of the effects of essentialism in the classroom. This pedagogical issue may well be the most urgent (and the most frustrating to resolve) since it speaks to the very subject of who can speak.

My strategy for approaching an already dangerously sedimented opposition in feminist thought is to work both sides of the essentialist/constructionist binarism at once, bringing each term to its interior breaking point. Such a bilateral approach does not presume, however, that it is possible to speak from a location above or beyond this powerful structuring opposition. My own position, throughout this text, is that of an anti-essentialist who wants to preserve (in both senses of the term: to maintain and to embalm) the category of essence. The complications and limitations as well as the possibilities and stratagems of this contradictory position will I hope become clear as the successive readings of essentialism unfold. Perhaps it only needs final emphasizing at this point that the project of interrogating essence wherever we may find it does not necessarily entail simultaneously dismissing it. By the same logic, to reach a clearer understanding of constructionism we must begin by recognizing and coming to terms with its internal contradictions. Simultaneously applying concentrated pressure to *both* sides of the binarism will yield a rather different set of conclusions about essentialism and constructionism than the prevalent appraisals of these heavily invested terms in critical discourse today, and it may offer a possible means, not to bypass, but to work through the many difficult, seemingly irresolvable debates this particular polemic inevitably seems to engender.

1

The "Risk" of Essence

One of the prime motivations behind the production of this book is the desire to break or in some way to weaken the hold which the essentialist/constructionist binarism has on feminist theory. It is my conviction that the deadlock created by the long-standing controversy over the issue of human essences (essential femininity, essential blackness, essential gayness . . .) has, on the one hand, encouraged more careful attention to cultural and historical specificities where perhaps we have hitherto been too quick to universalize but, on the other hand, foreclosed more ambitious investigations of specificity and difference by fostering a certain paranoia around the perceived threat of essentialism. It could be said that the tension produced by the essentialist/ constructionist debate is responsible for some of feminist theory's greatest insights, that is, the very tension is constitutive of the field of feminist theory. But it can also be maintained that this same dispute has created the current impasse in feminism, an impasse predicated on the difficulty of theorizing the social in relation to the natural, or the theoretical in relation to the political. The very confusion over whether or not the essentialist/constructionist tension is beneficial or detrimental to the health of feminism is itself overdetermined and constrained by the terms of the opposition in question.

One needs, therefore, to tread cautiously when mapping the boundaries of this important structuring debate for feminism. This chapter will begin by identifying the two key positions which are largely responsible for the current deadlock, and it will discuss some of the strengths and weaknesses of each position. One of the main contentions of this book is that essentialism, when held most under suspicion by constructionists, is often effectively doing its work elsewhere, under other guises, and sometimes laying the groundwork for its own critique. The bulk of the chapter will therefore address the way in which essentialism is *essential* to social constructionism, a point that powerfully

1

throws into question the stability and impermeability of the essentialist/
constructionist binarism. To this end I will look closely at currently
two of the most important and influential theories of anti-essentialism,
Lacanian psychoanalysis and Derridean deconstruction. In both cases
I intend to demonstrate the way in which the logic of essentialism can
be shown to be irreducible even in those discourses most explicitly
concerned with repudiating it.

Essentialism vs. Constructionism

Essentialism is classically defined as a belief in true essence—that
which is most irreducible, unchanging, and therefore constitutive of a
given person or thing. This definition represents the traditional Aristotelian understanding of essence, the definition with the greatest amount
of currency in the history of Western metaphysics.[1] In feminist theory,
essentialism articulates itself in a variety of ways and subtends a number of related assumptions. Most obviously, essentialism can be located
in appeals to a pure or original femininity, a female essence, outside
the boundaries of the social and thereby untainted (though perhaps
repressed) by a patriarchal order. It can also be read in the accounts
of universal female oppression, the assumption of a totalizing symbolic
system which subjugates all women everywhere, throughout history
and across cultures. Further, essentialism underwrites claims for the
autonomy of a female voice and the potentiality of a feminine language
(notions which find their most sophisticated expression in the much
discussed concept of *écriture féminine*).[2] Essentialism emerges perhaps
most strongly within the very discourse of feminism, a discourse which
presumes upon the unity of its object of inquiry (women) *even* when
it is at pains to demonstrate the differences within this admittedly
generalizing and imprecise category.

Constructionism, articulated in opposition to essentialism and concerned with its philosophical refutation, insists that essence is itself a
historical construction. Constructionists take the refusal of essence as
the inaugural moment of their own projects and proceed to demonstrate the way previously assumed self-evident kinds (like "man" or
"woman") are in fact the effects of complicated discursive practices.
Anti-essentialists are engaged in interrogating the intricate and interlac-
ing processes which work together to produce all seemingly "natural"
or "given" objects. What is at stake for a constructionist are systems
of representations, social and material practices, laws of discourses,
and ideological effects. In short, constructionists are concerned above
all with the *production* and *organization* of differences, and they there-

fore reject the idea that any essential or natural givens precede the processes of social determination.[3]

Essentialists and constructionists are most polarized around the issue of the relation between the social and the natural. For the essentialist, the natural provides the raw material and determinative starting point for the practices and laws of the social. For example, sexual difference (the division into "male" and "female") is taken as prior to social differences which are presumed to be mapped on to, *a posteriori*, the biological subject. For the constructionist, the natural is itself posited as a construction of the social. In this view, sexual difference is discursively produced, elaborated as an effect of the social rather than its *tabula rasa*, its prior object. Thus while the essentialist holds that the natural is *repressed* by the social, the constructionist maintains that the natural is *produced* by the social.[4] The difference in philosophical positions can be summed up by Ernest Jones's question: "Is woman born or made?" For an essentialist like Jones, woman is born not made; for an anti-essentialist like Simone de Beauvoir, woman is made not born.

Each of these positions, essentialism and constructionism, has demonstrated in the range of its deployment certain analytical strengths and weaknesses. The problems with essentialism are perhaps better known. Essentialist arguments frequently make recourse to an ontology which stands outside the sphere of cultural influence and historical change. "Man" and "woman," to take one example, are assumed to be ontologically stable objects, coherent signs which derive their coherency from their unchangeability and predictability (there have *always* been men and women it is argued). No allowance is made for the historical production of these categories which would necessitate a recognition that what the classical Greeks understood by "man" and "woman" is radically different from what the Renaissance French understood them to signify or even what the contemporary postindustrial, postmodernist, poststructuralist theoretician is likely to understand by these terms. "Man" and "woman" are not stable or universal categories, nor do they have the explanatory power they are routinely invested with. Essentialist arguments are not necessarily ahistorical, but they frequently theorize history as an unbroken continuum that transports, across cultures and through time, categories such as "man" and "woman" without in any way (re)defining or indeed (re)constituting them. History itself is theorized as essential, and thus unchanging; its essence is to generate change but not itself to *be* changed.

Constructionists, too, though they might make recourse to historicity as a way to challenge essentialism, nonetheless often work with uncomplicated or essentializing notions of history. While a constructionist might recognize that "man" and "woman" are produced across a spectrum of discourses, the categories "man" and "woman" still remain constant. Some minimal point of commonality and continuity necessitates at least the linguistic retention of these particular terms. The same problem emerges with the sign "history" itself, for while a constructionist might insist that we can only speak of *histories* (just as we can only speak of feminisms or deconstructionisms) the question that remains unanswered is what motivates or dictates the continued semantic use of the term "histories"? This is just one of many instances which suggest that essentialism is more entrenched in constructionism than we previously thought. In my mind, it is difficult to see how constructionism can *be* constructionism without a fundamental dependency upon essentialism.

It is common practice in social constructionist argumentation to shift from the singular to the plural in order to privilege heterogeneity and to highlight important cultural and social differences. Thus, woman becomes women, history becomes histories, feminism becomes feminisms, and so on. While this maneuver does mark a break with unitary conceptual categories (eternal woman, totalizing history, monolithic feminism), the hasty attempts to pluralize do not operate as sufficient defenses or safeguards against essentialism. The plural category "women," for instance, though conceptually signaling heterogeneity nonetheless semantically marks a collectivity; constructed or not, "women" still occupies the space of a linguistic unity. It is for this reason that a statement like "American women are 'x' " is no less essentializing than its formulation in the singular, "*The* American woman is 'x.' " The essentialism at stake is not countered so much as *displaced*.

If essentialism is more entrenched in constructionist logic than we previously acknowledged, if indeed there is no sure way to bracket off and to contain essentialist maneuvers in anti-essentialist arguments, then we must also simultaneously acknowledge that there is no essence to essentialism, that essence *as* irreducible has been *constructed* to be irreducible. Furthermore, if we can never securely displace essentialism, then it becomes useful for analytical purposes to distinguish between *kinds* of essentialisms, as John Locke has done with his theory of "real" versus "nominal" essence. Real essence connotes the Aristotelian understanding of essence as that which is most irreducible and unchanging about a thing; nominal essence signifies for Locke a view of essence as merely a linguistic convenience, a classificatory fiction we need to categorize and to label. Real essences are discovered by close empirical observation; nominal essences are not "discovered" so much as assigned or produced—produced specifically by language.[5] This specific distinction between real and nominal essence corresponds roughly to the broader oppositional categories of essentialism and constructionism: an essentialist assumes that innate or given essences sort objects naturally into species or kinds, whereas a constructionist assumes that it is language, the names arbitrarily affixed to objects, which establishes their existence in the mind. To clarify, a rose by any other name would still be a rose—for an essentialist; for a constructionist, a rose by any other name would not be a rose, it would be something altogether rather different.

Certainly, Locke's distinction between real and nominal essence is a useful one for making a political wedge into the essentialist/constructionist debate. When feminists today argue for maintaining the notion of a *class* of women, usually for political purposes, they do so I would suggest on the basis of Locke's nominal essence. It is Locke's distinction between nominal and real essence which allows us to work with the category of "women" as a *linguistic* rather than a natural kind, and for this reason Locke's category of nominal essence is especially useful for anti-essentialist feminists who want to hold onto the notion of women as a group without submitting to the idea that it is "nature" which categorizes them as such. And yet, however useful the "real" versus "nominal" classification may be for clarifying the relation between essence and language (transposing essence as an effect of language), the distinction it proposes is far from an absolute one. Real essence is itself a nominal essence—that is, a linguistic kind, a product of naming. And nominal essence is still an essence, suggesting that despite the circulation of different kinds of essences, they still all share a common classification *as essence*. I introduce the Lockean theory of essence to suggest both that it is crucial to discriminate between the ontological and linguistic orders of essentialism and that it is equally important to investigate their complicities as types of essentialisms, members of the same semantic family.

My point here, and throughout this book, is that social constructionists do not definitively escape the pull of essentialism, that indeed essentialism subtends the very idea of constructionism. Let me take another example, one often cited as the exemplary problem which separates the essentialist from the constructionist: the question of "the body." For the essentialist, the body occupies a pure, pre-social, pre-discursive space. The body is "real," accessible, and transparent; it is always *there* and directly interpretable through the senses. For the constructionist, the body is never simply there, rather it is composed of a network of effects continually subject to sociopolitical determination.

The body is "always already" culturally mapped; it never exists in a pure or uncoded state. Now the strength of the constructionist position is its rigorous insistence on the production of social categories like "the body" and its attention to systems of representation. But this strength is not built on the grounds of essentialism's demise, rather it works its power by strategically deferring the encounter with essence, displacing it, in this case, onto the concept of sociality.

To say that the body is always already deeply embedded in the social is not by any sure means to preclude essentialism. Essentialism is embedded in the idea of the social and lodged in the problem of social determination (and even, as I will later argue, directly implicated in the deconstructionist turn of phrase "always already"). Too often, constructionists presume that the category of the social automatically escapes essentialism, in contradistinction to the way the category of the natural is presupposed to be inevitably entrapped within it. But there is no compelling reason to assume that the natural is, in essence, essentialist and that the social is, in essence, constructionist. If we are to intervene effectively in the impasse created by the essentialist/ constructionist divide, it might be necessary to begin questioning the *constructionist* assumption that nature and fixity go together (naturally) just as sociality and change go together (naturally). In other words, it may be time to ask whether essences can change and whether constructions can be normative.

Lacanian Psychoanalysis

It has often been remarked that biological determinism and social determinism are simply two sides of the same coin: both posit an utterly passive subject subordinated to the shaping influence of either nature or culture, and both disregard the unsettling effects of the psyche.[6] There is a sense in which social constructionism can be unveiled as merely a form of sociological essentialism, a position predicated on the assumption that the subject is, in essence, a social construction. It may well be that at this particular historical moment it has become imperative to retrieve the subject from a total subordination to social determination. Perhaps that is why so many feminist theorists have turned to psychoanalysis as a more compelling, less essentializing account of the constructionist process. Psychoanalysis is in many ways the anti-essentialist discourse *par excellence* in that sexual difference is taken as something to be *explained* rather than assumed. But even psychoanalysis cannot do its work without making recourse to certain essentialist assumptions.

This is an important point since, next to deconstruction, psychoanalysis is generally the discourse most strongly identified as sufficiently able to repudiate metaphysical idealism and its reliance upon essentialism. Lacan refuses all treatments of the subject which take as self-evident an essential, pre-given identity; he is more concerned with displacing the classical humanist subject by demonstrating the production of the subject in language. I will have much more to say about Lacan's semiotic decentering of the subject in subsequent chapters, but for now I am interested in whether an account of the subject based on language can fully detach itself from the essentialist notions it claims so persistently to disinherit. I locate three main areas where Lacan leans heavily on essentialist underpinnings in order to advance an anti-essentialist argument: his emphasis on the speaking subject; his much heralded return to Freud; and, finally, his controversial theory of woman. Each of these points will be addressed in turn, but first it is imperative not to miss the point that constructionism is heavily indebted to Lacan for some of its greatest insights. Even a necessarily abbreviated account of Lacan's sophisticated and complex theory of the psyche will underscore the immense importance of his work for social constructionists.

Lacan's contribution to constructionism emerges out of his revision of some key Freudian concepts. For Freud, the Oedipus complex is the fundamental structure responsible for the formation of sexual identity in the child. But Lacan insists that while oedipal relations and the complicated processes of identification and desire they engender are crucial to the child's psychical development, the Oedipus complex is not a given but rather itself a problem to be elucidated through psychoanalytic inquiry. According to Lacan, Freud "falsifies the conception of the Oedipus complex from the start, by making it define as natural, rather than normative, the predominance of the paternal figure" ("Intervention on Transference," Mitchell and Rose 1982, 69). For Lacan the Oedipus complex is not biologically framed but symbolically cast; in fact, it is a product of that order which Lacan labels "the Symbolic." More specifically, the Symbolic represents the order of language which permits the child entry into subjectivity, into the realm of speech, law, and sociality. The Imaginary signifies the mother-child dyad which the Symbolic interrupts through the agency of the paternal function—the "Name-of-the-Father," rather than the biological father per se. Through this important shift from the father to the Name-of-the-Father, Lacan denaturalizes the Oedipal structure which Freud takes as universal, de-essentializes Freud's theory of subject constitution by opening it up to the play of language, symbol, and metaphor.

A second important point of revision which further positions Lacan as more "truly" anti-essentialist than Freud pertains to the role of the phallus in sexual differentiation. Here, too, Lacan faults his predecessor for failing to make the crucial distinction between anatomical organ (the penis) and representational symbol (the phallus). Freud repeatedly collapses the two, leaving himself vulnerable to charges of biologism and essentialism. Lacan is more careful to separate them, insisting that the phallus is not a fantasy, not an object, and most especially not an organ (the penis or the clitoris) ("The Meaning of the Phallus," Mitchell and Rose 1982, 79). The phallus is instead a *signifier*, a privileged signifier of the Symbolic order which may point to the penis as the most visible mark of sexual difference but nevertheless cannot be reduced to it. This non-coincidence of phallus and penis is important because "the relation of the subject to the phallus is set up regardless of the anatomical difference between the sexes" ("The Meaning of the Phallus," 76). In a sense, the phallus is *prior* to the penis; it is the privileged mark through which both sexes accede to sexual identity by a recognition and acceptance of castration.

There are a number of problems with Lacan's penis/phallus distinction which will be discussed here and at greater length in Chapter Four. To the extent that the phallus risks continually conjuring up images of the penis, that is, to the extent that the bar between these two terms cannot be rigidly sustained, Lacan is never very far from the essentialism he so vigorously disclaims. It is true that the phallus is *not* the penis in any simple way; as a signifier it operates as a sign in a signifying chain, a symbolic metaphor and not a natural fact of difference. But it is also true that this metaphor derives its power from the very object it symbolizes; the phallus is pre-eminently a metaphor but it is also metonymically close to the penis and derives much of its signifying importance from this by no means arbitrary relation. It is precisely because a woman does not have a penis that her relation to the phallus, the signifying order, the order of language and the law, is so complicated and fraught with difficulties. The privileging of the phallus as "transcendental signifier" (the signifier without a signified) has led to charges that Lacan is endorsing the phallocentrism he purports to critique. Luce Irigaray and Jacques Derrida have both detected in Lacan a perpetuation and strengthening of phallocentrism rather than its undoing.[7] This charge in turn has led to counter-charges that Lacan's detractors have confused the messenger with the message; at least two important defenders of Lacan, Juliet Flower MacCannell and Ellie Ragland-Sullivan, insist that Lacan is merely *describing* the effects of a phallocentric logic and not *prescribing* or in any way deploying them himself.[8] But in my mind these defenses are ultimately unconvincing, since "description" is never a pure form and can never escape a certain complicity with its object. Derrida, one of the first to take Lacan to task for the "phallogocentric transcendentalism" of his thinking, observes that "description is a 'participant' when it induces a practice, an ethics, and an institution, and therefore a politics that insure the truth of the tradition" (1980, 481). Such is the case with Lacan I would argue. But I must also add that despite Derrida's disclaimers that he has produced anything resembling a practice, an ethics, an institution, or a politics, Derridean deconstruction is no less "free" than Lacanian psychoanalysis from a pervasive albeit hidden (all the more pervasive because it is hidden) reliance upon essentialism. Both discourses profess to inhabit a theoretical space free of the taint of essentialism, but as I now hope to show, the very staking out of a *pure* anti-essentialist position simply reinscribes an inescapable essentialist logic.

While Lacan strategically employs linguistics to clean Freud's house of biologism, essentialism quietly returns to poststructuralist psycho-analysis through the back door, carried on the soles of Lacan's theory of signification. Lacan is careful to specify that when he says the subject is constituted in language, language does *not* signify for him mere social discourse. Lacan is here following Ferdinand de Saussure's de-scription of language as a system of relational signs, where meaning is a product of differences between signs and not an essential property of any fixed sign. Saussure makes a well-known distinction between "speech" and "language" in which speech (the individual communica-tion act) is "accidental" and language (the communal system of rules and codes which govern speech) is "essential" (1915, 14). Lacan, recognizing the inseparability of one from the other, sees both language and speech as "essential" to the founding of the human subject. For Lacan is first and foremost concerned with "the speaking subject" and with "the subjection of the subject to the signifier" ("The Subversion of the Subject and the Dialectic of Desire in the Freudian Unconscious" 1977, 304). In Lacanian psychoanalysis, speech is firmly inscribed as a discourse of truth; simply put, "speech connotes truth" ("The Func-tion and Field of Speech and Language in Psychoanalysis" 1977, 43).[9] The case can be stated even more strongly. What is irreducible to the discourse of psychoanalysis ("the talking cure") is speech. And, within the terms of this discourse, what is universal to psychoanalysis is the production of the subject *in the Symbolic*. From its institutional beginnings, psychoanalysis has relied upon "the function and field of speech and language" as its essential de-essentializing mechanisms of subject constitution, and (in Lacan's own words) it has taken as "self-evident fact that it deals solely with words" ("Intervention on Transference," Mitchell and Rose 1982, 63).

This brings us to the essentialism within Lacan's overall aim to return the institution of psychoanalysis to its authentic Freudian roots. Lacan's mission is to restore psychoanalysis to its essential truths, to what is most radical and irreducible about it. I must disagree with those commentators on Lacan who interpret his notion of a "return to Freud" as "merely a slogan."[10] Lacan's goal is to reinstate the truth of psychoanalysis, to recapture "the Freudian experience along authentic lines" ("Agency of the Letter in the Unconscious or Reason Since Freud" 1977, 171). The "return to Freud" may be in part a slogan (a rallying cry to turn psychoanalysis away from the distorted humanist appropriations of Freud by object-relations theorists and other post-Freudians) but it is also a symptom of Lacan's own complicity with an unacknowledged humanism (a sign of a certain susceptibility to the lure of meaning and Truth). In "The Freudian Thing, or the Meaning of the Return to Freud in Psychoanalysis," Lacan employs the logic of the chiasmus to argue that "the meaning of a return to Freud is a return to the meaning of Freud" (1977, 117). The "return to Freud" cannot be easily divorced from the notions of authenticity, recuperation, and truth-discourse which it repeatedly invokes. Perhaps it is this indissociability of the idea of return from the ideology of humanism which compels Lacan to acknowledge, at the end of the English selection of *Ecrits*, that it is humanism which marks the return of the repressed in his own work: "I must admit that I am partial to a certain form of humanism, a humanism that . . . has a certain quality of candour about it: 'When the miner comes home, his wife rubs him down . . .' I am left defenceless against such things" ("The Subversion of the Subject and the Dialectic of Desire in the Freudian Unconscious" 1977, 324).

The choice of a working-class couple (a wife attending to the material bodily needs of her miner-husband) to signal his "defencelessness" in the face of lived experience is an unusual example for Lacan, who generally makes few references in his work to class positions or material relations. This tendency points to an important vestige of essentialism in Lacan's theory of subjectivity: the assumption that the subject is raceless and classless. The Lacanian subject is a sexed subject first and last; few allowances are made for the way in which other modes of difference might complicate or even facilitate the account of identity formation Lacan outlines along the axis of sex alone. Within the specific realm of sexual differentiation, essentialism emerges most strongly in Lacan's very attempts to displace the essence of "woman." Of real material women, such as the miner's wife, Lacan has nothing to say, readily admits his knowing ignorance. But of "woman" as sign Lacan has everything to say (especially since women, as we shall see, cannot say "it" themselves).

In Seminar XX, devoted to the enigma of woman and the riddle of femininity, Lacan tells us that woman, as such, does not exist:

> when any speaking being whatever lines up under the banner of women it is by being constituted as not all that they are placed within the phallic function. It is this that defines the . . . the what?—the woman precisely, except that *The* woman can only be written with *The* crossed through. There is no such thing as *The* woman, where the definite article stands for the universal. ("God and the *Jouissance* of T̶h̶e̶ Woman," Mitchell and Rose 1982, 144)

On the surface, Lacan's erasure of the "The" in "The woman" is a calculated effort to de-essentialize woman. Eternal Woman, the myth of Woman, Transcendental Woman—all are false universals for Lacan, held in place only by the dubious efforts of the "signifier which cannot signify anything"—the definite article "the" ("God and the *Jouissance* of T̶h̶e̶ Woman," 144). But is Lacan's mathematical "woman" (in "Seminar of 21 January 1975" he describes woman as an "empty set") any less universalizing than the metaphysical notion of woman he seeks to challenge? Essence quickly reappears as a "risk" Lacan cannot resist taking: "There is no such thing as *The* woman since of her essence— having already risked the term, why think twice about it?—of her essence, she is not all" ("God and the *Jouissance* of T̶h̶e̶ Woman," 144). The project to de-essentialize "woman" is activated on the grounds of simultaneously re-essentializing her. The "risk" lies in the double gesture, the very process of transgressing the essentialist/constructionist divide.

In defining the essence of woman as "not all," the penis/phallus distinction once again comes into play, but this time as a way to keep essentialism in place. "It is through the phallic function that man takes up his inscription as all," Lacan explains in "A Love Letter" (Mitchell and Rose 1982, 150). All speaking beings are allowed to place themselves on the side of the not all, on the side of woman. Woman's supplementary *jouissance*, a *jouissance* "beyond the phallus," is "proper" to biological women but not exclusive to them. Men (specifically male mystics for Lacan) can also occupy the subject-position "woman"; in fact, "there are men who are just as good as women. It does happen" ("God and the *Jouissance* of T̶h̶e̶ Woman," 147). But, importantly, the converse is not true for Lacan: not all speaking beings are allowed to inscribe themselves on the side of the all, since only men have penises which give them more direct access to "the phallic function." Exclusion from *total* access to the Symbolic's privileged transcendental signifier has certain implications for the already castrated woman, not the least of which is a highly problematized relation to speech and language. "There is woman only as excluded by the nature of things which is the nature of words" we are told ("God and the *Jouissance* of The Woman," 144). Speaking specifically of woman's *jouissance* beyond the phallus, Lacan can only conclude that it is "impossible to tell whether the woman can say anything about it— whether she can say what she knows of it" ("A Love Letter," 159).

Derrida's attempts to speak (as) woman have provoked considerable controversy, but little has been said of Lacan's perhaps more veiled attempts to do the same. Desire *for* the Other often manifests itself as desire to speak as Other, from the place of the Other (some would even say, *instead* of the Other). I read Lacan's difficult and equivocal style not just as a strategic evocation of the laws of the Unconscious (which is how it is usually understood) but also, since woman is presumed to be closer to the Unconscious, as an attempt to approximate the speech-less, the not all, the elusive figure of Woman who personifies Truth. Through the device of the quotation marks, Lacan literally assumes the voice of Woman/Truth in "The Freudian Thing" (1977, esp. 121–23). But in a more general way, through the evasive and elliptical style which is his trademark, Lacan attempts to bring woman to the point of speech by approximating the vanishing point in his own speech. In his theory of woman as "not all," Lacan posits the essence of woman as an enigmatic excess or remainder. In this regard, woman remains for Lacan the enigma she was for Freud. In fact, essence operates in Lacan as a leftover classical component which re-emerges in his theory of woman precisely because it is woman who escapes complete subjection to the Symbolic and its formative operations. In her inscription as not all (as Truth, lack, Other, *objet a*, God) woman becomes for Lacan the very repository of essence.

Derridean Deconstruction

And what of Derrida's theory of essence? Does Derrida "transcend" essentialism more successfully than Lacan, and if not, where is it inscribed and what implications might it hold for the most rigorous anti-essentialist discourse of all: deconstruction? My position here is that the possibility of any radical constructionism can only be built on the foundations of a hidden essentialism. Derrida would, of course, be quick to agree that despite the dislocating effects of deconstruction's strategies of reversal/displacement we can never get beyond metaphysics, and therefore, since all of Western metaphysics is predicated upon Aristotle's essence/accident distinction, we can never truly get beyond essentialism. This is why we should not be surprised to see certain metaphysical holds operative in Derrida's own work, supporting even his relentless pursuit of binary oppositions and phenomenological essences. My interest in exploring what Derrida calls "fringes of irreducibility" (1972c, 67) as they operate in deconstruction itself is motivated not by a desire to demonstrate that Derrida is a *failed* constructionist (this would be a pointless exercise, given the terms of my argument) but by an interest in uncovering the ways in which deconstruction deploys essentialism against itself, leans heavily on essence in its determination to displace essence. Derrida's theory of woman is one place to start, though as I hope to show, essentialism works its logic through a number of important "Derrideanisms," including the emphasis upon undecidability and the related notions of contradiction and heterogeneity.

Woman and undecidability are, in fact, rather closely linked in Derrida's work. This intimate association is most evident in *Spurs* (1978) where Derrida attempts to come to grips with the question "What is woman?" through a sustained reading of the inscription of woman in Nietzsche's philosophy. Woman occupies for Nietzsche the site of a contradiction: she represents both truth and non-truth, distance and proximity, wisdom and deceit, authenticity and simulation. But Derrida points out that woman can be none of these things, in essence, since "there is no such thing as a woman, as a truth in itself of woman in itself" (101). Like Lacan, Derrida's project is to displace the essence of woman, but also like Lacan, Derrida is actively engaged in the redeployment of essentialism elsewhere. For Derrida, woman operates as the very figure of undecidability. It is woman as undecidable variable who displaces the rigid dualisms of Western metaphysics: "The question of the woman suspends the decidable opposition of true and non-true and inaugurates the epochal regime of quotation marks which is to be enforced for every concept belonging to the system of philosophical decidability" (107). Woman, in short, is yet another figure for *différance*, the mechanism which undoes and disables "ontological decidability" (111). But more than this, she is the non-place which centers deconstruction's own marginal status in philosophical discourse. When Gayatri Spivak identifies the phenomenon of woman's "double displacement" in deconstruction, she is referring to the tendency of deconstruction to announce its own displacement by situating woman as a figure of displacement (see Spivak 1983 and Spivak 1984). While there may be nothing essentialistic about this maneuver *per se*, one at least has to recognize that positing woman as a figure of displacement risks, in its effects, continually displacing real material women.

"Choreographies" (1982) extends Derrida's critique of the essence of woman by warning against the dangers of seeking to locate and to identify "woman's place": "in my view there is no one place for woman. It is without a doubt risky to say that there is no place for woman, but this idea is not anti-feminist . . ." (68). There is an interesting slippage here from the claim that "there is no one place for woman" to the claim that "there is no place for woman"—two rather different statements indeed. But Derrida's point seems to be simply that a "woman's place," a single place, must necessarily be essentializing. This is doubtless true, but we need to ask whether positing multiple places for women is necessarily any *less* essentializing. Does "woman's *places*" effectively challenge the unitary, metaphysical notion of the subject/ woman who presumably fills these particular places and not others? Derrida also makes the claim in "Choreographies" that there is no essence of woman, at least no "essence which is rigorously or properly identifiable" (72). Here one sees more clearly the opening for essentialism's re-entry onto the stage of deconstruction, for in the end Derrida does not so much challenge that woman has an essence as insist that we can never "rigorously" or "properly" identify it. Woman's essence is simply "undecidable," a position which frequently inverts itself in deconstruction to the suggestion that it is the essence of woman to *be* the undecidable. To say that woman's essence is to be the undecidable is different from claiming that woman's essence is undecidable and different still from claiming that it is undecidable whether woman has an essence at all. Derrida's theory of essence moves between and among these contradictory positions, playing upon the undecidability and ambiguity which underwrites his own deconstructionist maneuvers.

Let me shift focus then to deconstruction itself and to its decisive encounter with Husserlian phenomenology. It is by no means insignificant that Derrida's earliest published pieces manifest a preoccupation with essentialism and especially with the place of essence in phenomenology. Phenomenology is defined in Husserl's *Logical Investigations* (1901) as the study of the essence of human consciousness. Essence is not a question of empirical investigation but rather a matter of pure abstractions—the very foundation of logic and mathematics. A case is made by Husserl for "an *a priori* necessity of essence" (443); objects are seen to have "pure essences" which are self-evidently true—"nonempirical, universal, and unconditionally valid" (446). Husserl believed that by removing essence from the empirical realm of natural science and relocating it in the universal realm of pure logic he was achieving a radical break with metaphysics. Essence, in this early twentieth-century phenomenological view, is not something that lies behind a given thing, but rather essence is that which is most *self-evident* and *self-given* about that thing: a figure is, in essence, a triangle if the sum of its angles add up to 180 degrees. In Husserlian phenomenology, then, it is self-evidence which operates as the basis of epistemology, the validation of the truth of all knowledge.

Derrida explicitly takes on the project to displace phenomenological essence in several of his early works, including *Speech and Phenomena* (1967b),[11] and his aim is what we have now come to see as characteristically Derridean: "to see the phenomenological critique of metaphysics betray itself as a moment within the history of metaphysical assurance" (1967b, 5). Because transcendental phenomenology is rooted in the idea of *givenness*, Derrida's tactic is to apply enough analytical pressure to the concept of self-evidence to pry open phenomenology's deeply rooted investments with metaphysics. To the extent that Husserl's work aspires to be a science of essence, phenomenology emerges not as metaphysics' most radical subversion but as its most successful reinscription. Phenomenology, Derrida shows, seeks not only to preserve the central place of essence in metaphysics, it also seeks to return metaphysics to its own essence—its essence as "first philosophy." Derrida's critique of Husserl's epistemology of essences is a particularly persuasive one, for he convincingly demonstrates that essences, as Husserl understands them, are pre-cultural and atemporal and therefore inescapably ontological.[12]

In yet another twist of the metaphysical screw, deconstruction itself can only sustain its project to undo the normative operations of phenomenal essences by activating the "philosopheme" of essence under other, less obvious guises. Essence manifests itself in deconstruction in that most pervasive, most recognizable of Derridean phrases, "always already" (*toujours déjà*).[13] This phrase marks a phenomenological carryover in Derrida's work, a point of refuge for essentialism which otherwise, in deconstruction, comes so consistently under attack. It is my belief that "always already" frequently appears at those points where Derrida wishes to put the brakes on the analysis in progress and to make a turn in another direction. Occurrences of "always already" (or sometimes its abbreviated form "always") function as stop signs that alert us to some of Derrida's central assumptions—for example, his assumption in "Racism's Last Word" that the name "apartheid" is not merely the "last word" but also the first word of racism: "hasn't *apartheid* always been the archival record of the unnameable?" (1985a, 291) Importantly, the controversy and debate which has surrounded Derrida's piece on apartheid rests heavily on this seemingly innocent and innocuous little word, "always." Consider Anne McClintock and Rob Nixon's much debated materialist response to Derrida's "Racism's Last Word":

> When Derrida asks, "Hasn't *apartheid* always been the archival re-cord of the unnameable?" (p. 291), the answer is a straightforward no. Despite its notoriety and currency overseas, the term *apartheid* has not always been the "watchword" of the Nationalist regime (p. 291). It has its own history, and that history is closely entwined with a developing ideology of race. ("No Names Apart: The Separation of Word and History in Derrida's 'Le Dernier Mot du Racisme' " 1986, 141)

What Nixon and McClintock are objecting to is the idealism in Derri-da's work, the "severance of word from history" (141). Not only do I believe that there is some basis for such a claim, I would also maintain that it is the use of the term "always" which operates as the hidden trip wire which captures the word *apartheid* in the prison house of language. Yet Derrida himself objects strongly to the charge that he has failed to historicize properly the word *apartheid*, and he objects on the grounds that Nixon and McClintock have merely substituted *their* version of "always" for *his* version of "always"—in other words, that it is they, and not he, who have taken the contested word out of its proper context:

> Once again you mistake the most evident meaning of my question. It did not concern the use of the word *by* the Nationalist regime but its *use value* in the world, "its notoriety and currency overseas," as you so rightly put it. The word "always" in my text referred to this notoriety and there is little matter here for disagreement. But I never said that *apartheid* has "always" been the *literal* "watchword" *within* the Nationalist regime. And I find the way you manage to slip the "always" out of *my* sentence ("but hasn't *apartheid* always been the archival record of the unnameable?") and into *yours* ("the term *apartheid* has not always been the 'watchword' of the Nationalist regime") to be less than honest. To be honest, you would have had to quote the whole sentence in which I myself speak of the "watchword" as such. ("But, beyond . . . [Open Letter to Anne Mc-Clintock and Rob Nixon]" 1986, 160)

No one can turn a criticism back upon his opponents more dexterously and more dramatically than Derrida, and yet I am compelled to wonder why Derrida thinks his use of the term "always" is *more* "self-evident" than Nixon and McClintock's; there is a not so subtle presumption here that Nixon and McClintock have bastardized the term "always" by reading it historically, temporally, "literally"—sullied its purer metaphorical, indeed *metaphysical*, connotations with less sophisticated materialist trappings.

A danger implicit in the ready application of the logic of *toujours déjà* is the temptation to rely upon the "always already" self-evident "nature" of "always already." The fact that "always already" is a phrase that has been so readily appropriated (and on occasion parodied) in academic circles immediately casts suspicion on its efficacy. At the present moment, "always already" has such wide currency amongst poststructuralists and non-poststructuralists alike that it has lost much of the rhetorical power and energy which characterizes its appearances in Derrida's work. Consider Houston Baker's otherwise suggestive discussion of the blues as "the multiplex enabling *script* in which Afro-American cultural discourse is inscribed" (1984, 4). In *Blues, Ideology, and Afro-American Literature: A Vernacular Theory* (1984), Baker identifies the blues as the central trope in Afro-American culture, but exactly why the blues have come to function as the *primary* "script" of Afro-American literature is by no means clear. Just when we expect an explanation from Baker on his choice of the blues, he tells us that "they are what Jacques Derrida might describe as the 'always already' of Afro-American culture" (4). But why the blues? Why not, as at least one other critic of Afro-American culture has wondered, "spirituals, jubilees, hollers, work songs . . . or jazz" (Tracy 1985, 100)? Or why not, for that matter, an expressive cultural form *other* than music? Baker's invocation of "always already" is a surprising moment in a context which clearly demands historicization; while the specificity of the blues genre is rigorously historicized in Baker's text, the *choice* of the blues (as the very quintessence of Afro-American expressive culture) curiously is not. The danger (and the usefulness) of "always already" is that it *implies* essence, it hints at an irreducible core that requires no further investigation. In so doing, it frequently puts a stop to analysis, often at an argument's most critical point.

In Derrida's work "always already" operates as something of a contradiction: it arrests analysis at a crucial stage, but it also shifts analytical gears and moves us along in another direction, much like the "switch engines" of one of Baker's railway roundhouses. It is a technique which deliberately frustrates closure and keeps meaning in play; but it is also a technique that relies upon the self-evidence of contradiction and heterogeneity. In his response to Nixon and McClintock, we see that what gets fetishized in Derrida's work is precisely this notion of contradiction:

> Far from relying on "monoliths" or "bulky homogeneities," I constantly emphasize heterogeneity, contradictions, tensions, and uneven development. "Contradiction" is the most frequently occurring word in my text. (165)

By my count (since we seem to be engaged in a numbers game here), the most frequently occurring word (noun?) in Derrida's "Racism's Last Word" is not "contradiction" but "apartheid." Could we not say that, within the terms of Derrida's investigation, "apartheid" has been symptomatically erased by "contradiction," and is this not Nixon and McClintock's point in the end? "Contradiction" emerges as the "always already" of deconstruction, its irreducible inner core without which it could not do its work. It is *essential* to deconstruction, and as such it runs the risk of reification and solidification, a point that Derrida seems elsewhere to be fully aware of ("Différance," for example) and yet here he does not hesitate to summon contradiction's unassailable power to silence his critics. After citing the many instances in which he spoke of contradiction in "Racism's Last Word," Derrida writes, angrily: "Is that a sign of monolithic thinking and a preference for homogeneity? This will surely have been the first time I have met with such a reproach, and I fear you deserve it more than I do" (165). Derrida holds a mirror up to his detractors and reflects their charges of "monolithic thinking" and "homogeneity" back to them, unwilling to recognize any possible contradictions within his own discourse, willing only (in surprisingly unDerridean fashion) to treat contradiction on a thematic level and not on a deeper textual level.

"The risk of essence may have to be taken"

Despite the uncertainty and confusion surrounding the sign "essence," more than one influential theorist has advocated that perhaps we cannot do without recourse to irreducibilities. One thinks of Stephen Heath's by now famous suggestion, "the risk of essence may have to be taken" ("Difference" 1978, 99). It is poststructuralist feminists who seem most intrigued by this call to risk essence. Alice Jardine, for example, finds Stephen Heath's proclamation (later echoed by Gayatri Spivak) to be "one of the most thought-provoking statements of recent date" ("Men in Feminism: Odor di Uomo Or Compagnons de Route?" in Jardine and Smith 1987, 58). But not all poststructuralist feminists are as comfortable with the prospect of re-opening theory's Pandora's box of essentialism. Peggy Kamuf warns that calls to risk essentialism may in the end be no more than veiled defenses against the unsettling operations of deconstruction:

> How is one supposed to understand essence as a *risk* to be run when it is by definition the non-accidental and therefore hardly the apt term to represent danger or risk? Only over against and in impatient reaction to the deconstruction of the subject can "essence" be made to sound excitingly dangerous and the phrase "the risk of essence" can seem to offer such an appealing invitation. . . . "Go for it," the phrase incites. "If you fall into 'essence,' you can always say it was an accident." ("Femmeninism," in Jardine and Smith 1987, 96)

In Kamuf's mind, risking essence is really no risk at all; it is merely a clever way of preserving the metaphysical safety net should we lose our balance walking the perilous tightrope of deconstruction.

But the call to risk essence is not merely an "impatient reaction" to deconstruction (though it might indeed be this in certain specific instances); it can also operate as a deconstructionist strategy. "Is not strategy itself the real risk?" Derrida asks in his seminar on feminism ("Women in the Beehive," in Jardine and Smith 1987, 192). To the deconstructionist, strategy of any kind is a risk because its effects, its outcome, are always unpredictable and undecidable. Depending on the historical moment and the cultural context, a strategy can be "radically revolutionary or deconstructive" or it can be "dangerously reactive" (193). What is risky is giving up the security—and the fantasy—of occupying a single subject-position and instead occupying two places at once. In a word, "we have to negotiate" (202). For an example of this particular notion of "risk" we can turn to Derrida's own attempts to dare to speak as woman. For a male subject to speak as woman can be radically de-essentializing; the transgression suggests that "woman" is a social space which any sexed subject can fill. But because Derrida never specifies *which* woman he speaks as (a French bourgeois woman, an Anglo-American lesbian, and so on), the strategy to speak as woman is simultaneously re-essentializing. The risk lies in the difficult negotiation between these apparently contradictory effects.

It must be pointed out here that the constructionist strategy of specifying more precisely these sub-categories of "woman" does not necessarily preclude essentialism. "French bourgeois woman" or "Anglo-American lesbian," while crucially emphasizing in their very specificity that "woman" is by no means a monolithic category, nonetheless reinscribe an essentialist logic at the very level of historicism. Historicism is not always an effective counter to essentialism if it succeeds only in fragmenting the subject into multiple identities, each with its own self-contained, self-referential essence. The constructionist impulse to specify, rather than definitively counteracting essentialism, often simply redeploys it through the very strategy of historicization, rerouting and dispersing it through a number of micropolitical units or sub-categorical classifications, each presupposing its own unique interior composition or metaphysical core.

There is an important distinction to be made, I would submit, between "deploying" or "activating" essentialism and "falling into" or "lapsing into" essentialism. "Falling into" or "lapsing into" implies that essentialism is inherently reactionary—inevitably and inescapably a problem or a mistake.[14] "Deploying" or "activating," on the other hand, implies that essentialism may have some strategic or interventionary value. What I am suggesting is that the political investments of the sign "essence" are predicated on the subject's complex positioning in a particular social field, and that the appraisal of this investment depends not on any interior values intrinsic to the sign itself but rather on the shifting and determinative discursive relations which produced it. As subsequent chapters will more forcefully suggest, the radicality or conservatism of essentialism depends, to a significant degree, on *who* is utilizing it, *how* it is deployed, and *where* its effects are concentrated.

It is important not to forget that essence is a sign, and as such historically contingent and constantly subject to change and to redefinition. Historically, we have never been very confident of the definition of essence, nor have we been very certain that the definition of essence is to *be* the definitional. Even the essence/accident distinction, the inaugural moment of Western metaphysics, is by no means a stable or secure binarism. The entire history of metaphysics can be read as an interminable pursuit of the essence of essence, motivated by the anxiety that essence may well be accidental, changing and unknowable. Essentialism is not, and has rarely been, monolithically coded. Certainly it is difficult to identify a single philosopher whose work does not attempt to account for the question of essentialism in some way; the repeated attempts by these philosophers to fix or to define essence suggest that essence is a slippery and elusive category, and that the sign itself does not remain stationary or uniform.

The deconstruction of essentialism, rather than putting essence to rest, simply raises the discussion to a more sophisticated level, leaps the analysis up to another higher register, above all, keeps the sign of essence in play, even if (indeed *because*) it is continually held under erasure. Constructionists, then, need to be wary of too quickly crying "essentialism." Perhaps the most dangerous problem for anti-essentialists is to see the category of essence as "always already" knowable, as immediately apparent and naturally transparent. Similarly, we need to beware of the tendency to "naturalize" the category of the natural, to see this category, too, as obvious and immediately perceptible *as such*. Essentialism may be at once more intractable and more irrecuperable than we thought; it may be essential to our thinking while at the same time there is nothing "quintessential" about it. To insist that essentialism is always and everywhere reactionary is, for the constructionist, to buy into essentialism in the very act of making the charge; *it is to act as if essentialism has an essence.*

2

Reading Like a Feminist

In light of the pervasive reluctance amongst poststructuralists to acknowledge any possible productive role for essentialism, the issue of constructionism's complicity with essentialism demands more careful and precise demonstration. Let me pose the central problematic in a slightly different way: can social constructionism entirely dispense with the idea of essence? In this chapter I propose not to confront the stronghold of constructionism head-on, as I attempted to do in the previous chapter, but to take a more oblique approach by engaging with the subsidiary debates on gender and reading. What does it mean to read as a woman or as a man? When social constructionist theories of reading posit groups of gendered readers, what is it exactly that underwrites and subtends the notion of a class of women or a class of men reading? Precisely *where*, in other words, does the essentialism inhere in anti-essentialism? Although the present analysis focuses predominantly upon three recent pieces, Robert Scholes's "Reading Like a Man" (1987), Tania Modleski's "Feminism and the Power of Interpretation" (1986), and Gayatri Spivak's "Subaltern Studies: Deconstructing Historiography" (1987), the dispute over "reading as woman" has a much longer history which includes Peggy Kamuf's "Writing Like a Woman" (1980), Jonathan Culler's "Reading as a Woman" (1982), and, most recently, the many contributions to the controversial volume *Men in Feminism* (Jardine and Smith 1987). In the background of all these investigations lies the question of essentialism and the problem of the vexed relation between feminism and deconstruction. How and why have the current tensions between feminism and deconstruction mobilized around the issue of essentialism? Why indeed is essentialism such a powerful and seemingly intransigent category for both deconstructionists and feminists? Is it possible to be an essentialist deconstructionist, when deconstruction is commonly understood as the very displacement of essence? By the same token, is it legitimate to call oneself an anti-essentialist feminist, when feminism seems to take for granted among its members a shared identity, some essential point of commonality?

Essence, Experience, and Empowerment

According to one well-known American critic, feminism and deconstruction are fundamentally incompatible discourses since deconstruction displaces the essence of the class "women" which feminism needs to articulate its very politics. The polarization of feminism and deconstruction around the contested sign of essence is perhaps nowhere so clear as in Robert Scholes's "Reading Like a Man," a piece which seeks to disclose the often subtle and frequently suspect strategies which, in this instance, (male?) deconstructors employ to master feminism and to put it in its place. I find Scholes's careful critique of Jonathan Culler's "Reading as a Woman" both incisive and enormously suggestive, but not entirely devoid of certain mastering strategies of its own. It is these strategies that I wish to discuss here, while declaring all the same my fundamental agreement with Scholes's basic premise that the relation between deconstruction and feminism is by no means unproblematic or uncomplicated. The most serious (but also the most intriguing) problem with this essay is that it leaves the feminism/deconstruction binarism firmly in place—it reinforces and solidifies their antithesis in order to claim that deconstruction is bad for feminism. To secure this moral judgment, the hybrid positions of deconstructive feminism and feminist deconstruction are glossed over, rejected from the start as untenable possibilities—untenable because feminism and deconstruction are "founded upon antithetical principles: feminism upon a class concept and deconstruction upon the deconstructing of all such concepts" (208).

Everything hinges here, as Scholes himself is quick to point out, on the notion of "class." What he objects to, specifically, is deconstruction's rejection of what W. K. Wimsatt, following Locke, calls "nominal universality" (208), that is, nominal essence. Nominal essence, as we recall, refers to the ranking and labeling of things not according to the real essence in them but the complex ideas in us. Scholes believes that feminism needs at least to hold onto the logico-linguistic idea of a class of women in order to be effective. I would not disagree. I would, however, wish to point out that nominal essences are often treated by post-Lockeans *as if* they were real essences, and this is what I perceive to be the main point of vulnerability in "Reading Like a Man." While still subscribing to the "linguistic/logical dimension" of class, Scholes later goes on to endorse "the ability of women to be conscious of themselves as a class . . . bound by a certain shared experience" (212–13). What, then, does the category "experience" signify for Scholes? "Whatever experience is," he concludes, "it is not just a *construct* but something that *constructs*" (215). This definition sounds remarkably similar to Locke's description of "real essence" as the "something I know not what" which nonetheless determines the "what" of who we are. And what is it, exactly, that constitutes that "certain shared experience" which allows women "to be conscious of themselves as a class"? Could it be that which Scholes reprimands Culler for eliding, precisely that which Culler (in Scholes's opinion) rashly jettisons from consideration in his deconstructive third moment: namely, "the bodily experience of menstrual flow" (211)? Of course, not all females, in fact, menstruate. It may well be that Scholes wishes us to think of "experience" in the way Teresa de Lauretis suggests: "an on-going process by which subjectivity is constructed semiotically and historically" (1984, 182).

But what distinguishes Scholes's understanding of experience from de Lauretis's is the former's hidden appeal to referentiality, to (in this case) the female body, which though constructed is nonetheless constructed *by its own processes*, processes which are seen to be real, immediate, and directly knowable.[1] Bodily experiences may seem self-evident and immediately perceptible but they are always socially mediated. Even if we were to agree that experience is not merely constructed but also itself constructing, we would still have to acknowledge that there is little agreement amongst women on exactly what constitutes "a woman's experience." Therefore, we need to be extremely wary of the temptation to make substantive claims on the basis of the so-called "authority" of our experiences. "No man should seek in any way to diminish the authority which the experience of women gives them in speaking about that experience" (217–18), Scholes insists, and yet, as feminist philosopher Jean Grimshaw rightly reminds us, "experience does not come neatly in segments, such that it is always possible to abstract what in one's experience is due to 'being a woman' from that which is due to 'being married,' 'being middle class' and so forth" (1986, 85). In sum, "experience" is rather shaky ground on which to base the notion of a class of women. But if we can't base the idea of a class of women on "essence" or "experience," then what can we base it on? Before tendering a possible answer to what is admittedly a vexing and frustrating question, much more needs to be said by way of rounding out my critique of Scholes's "Reading Like a Man."

By taking as his model of feminism a humanist or essentialist version, and by reading deconstruction as fundamentally anti-essentialist, Scholes forecloses the possibility of both an anti-essentialist feminism and an essentialist deconstruction. But recent work in feminist theory suggests that not only are these positions possible, they can be powerfully displacing positions from which feminists can speak. To take the first instance, an anti-essentialist feminism, Monique Wittig rejects unequivocally the idea of a "class of women" based on shared (biological) experience and bases her feminism on the deconstructive premise that, in Derrida's words, "woman has no essence of her very own" (1985b, 31). To take the second instance, an essentialist deconstruction, Luce Irigaray bases her feminism on the bodily metaphor of "the two lips" in order to construct and *deconstruct* "woman" at the same time. Both of these feminist theorists will be discussed in greater detail in the following chapters; what I wish to emphasize here is that Scholes's feminism/deconstruction binarism is ultimately more harmful than helpful. It leads, for example, to such baffling statements as "feminism is right and deconstruction is wrong" (205). Mastery, in Scholes's work, operates along an ethical axis: feminism is disappropriated from deconstruction so that its alleged moral superiority might be protected from the ill repute and questionable designs of its powerful (male?) suitor, deconstruction. What we see in this piece is a curious form of critical chivalry; feminism, I would submit, has become the angel in the house of critical theory.

But who is this errant knight dedicated to saving feminism, and from what country does he heed? what language does he speak? Does Scholes speak, read, or write as a woman or as a man? The final lines provide the answer we have all eagerly been waiting for:

> We are subjects constructed by our experience and truly carry traces of that experience in our minds and on our bodies. Those of us who are male cannot deny this either. With the best will in the world we shall never read as women and perhaps not even like women. For me, born when I was born and living where I have lived, the very best I can do is to be conscious of the ground upon which I stand: to read not as but like a man. (218)

The distinction between the similes "as" and "like" is nothing short of brilliant, but it does not answer a far more interesting question, a question which, through a series of rather nimble acrobatic maneuvers of his own, Scholes manages to sidestep: namely, does he read as or like a *feminist*? It is the very slippages between "woman," "women," "female," and "feminist" throughout the text that permits the writer to defer the question of reading as or like a feminist—the question, in other words, of *political identification*. I read this piece *like* a feminist; what it means to read as or even like a woman I still don't know.

Scholes is not alone in his repudiation of Jonathan Culler's alleged deconstructionist appropriation of feminism; Tania Modleski, in her "Feminism and the Power of Interpretation: Some Critical Readings" also takes Culler to task for "being patriarchal just at the point when he seems to be most feminist," that is, at the point "when he arrogates to himself and to other male critics the ability to read as women by 'hypothesizing' women readers" (133). What allows a male subject to read as a woman is the displacing series of repetitions which Culler adapts from Peggy Kamuf's "Writing Like a Woman": "a woman writing as a woman writing as a woman. . . ." But, to Modleski, the deconstructionist definition of a woman reading (as a woman reading as a woman . . .) simply opens a space for male feminism while simultaneously foreclosing the question of real, material female readers: "a genuinely feminist literary criticism might wish to repudiate the *hypothesis* of a woman reader and instead promote the 'sensible,' visible, actual female reader" (133). While I am not contesting that there are certainly "real," material, gendered readers engaged in the act of reading, I nonetheless stumble over the qualifier "genuinely": what is it, exactly, that might constitute for Modleski a "genuinely feminist literary criticism"?

Read alongside Scholes's "Reading Like a Man," Modleski's "Feminism and the Power of Interpretation" proposes an answer that should perhaps not surprise us: "the experience of real women" (134) operates as the privileged signifier of the authentic and the real. Experience emerges to fend off the entry of men into feminism and, further, to naturalize and to authorize the relation between biological woman and social women: "to read as a woman in a patriarchal culture necessitates that the *hypothesis* of a woman reader be advanced by an *actual* woman reader: the female feminist critic" (133–134). Like Scholes, Modleski can appeal to experience as the measure of the "genuinely feminist" only by totally collapsing woman, female, and feminist and by prefacing this tricky conflation with the empirical tag "actual." Modleski objects to Kamuf's and Culler's ostensible position that "a 'ground' (like experience) from which to make critical judgments is anathema" (134). If this were an accurate assessment of Kamuf's and Culler's positions I might be inclined to agree, but the poststructuralist objection to experience is not a repudiation of grounds of knowing *per se* but rather a refusal of the hypostatization of experience as *the* ground (and the most stable ground) of knowledge production. The problem with categories like "the female experience" or "the male experience" is that, given their generality and seamlessness, they are of limited epistemological usefulness. When Modleski does some hypothesizing of her own and presents us with her fictional "case of a man and a woman reading Freud's text," and when she informs us (without a hint of irony) that "the woman, accustomed to the experience of being thought more sensual than intellectual, must certainly respond to it differently from the man . . ." (133), what "woman" and what "man" is she talking about? Can we ever speak so simply of "the female reader" or "the male reader" (133), "the woman" and "the man," as if these categories were not transgressed, not already constituted by other axes of difference (class, culture, ethnicity, nationality . . .)? Moreover, are our reading responses really so easily predictable, so readily interpretable?

Both Modleski and Scholes are right to insist that critical interpretation has everything to do with power. Why, then, do I find Modleski's concluding invocation of "female empowerment" so distinctly *disempowering*? Her words are strong, emphatic, a political call to arms: "the ultimate goal of feminist criticism and theory is female empowerment. My particular concern here has been to empower female readers of texts, in part by rescuing them from the oblivion to which some critics would consign them" (136). Perhaps what is discomforting is the singular, declarative, and prescriptive tone of this guideline for political action. But it is more than a question of tone. Exactly which readers is Modleski speaking for, to, and about? Does she propose to rescue *all* female readers, including "third world" readers, lesbian readers, and working-class readers? Are not some female readers *materially* more empowered than others, by virtue of class, race, national, or other criteria? For that matter, are not *some* female readers more empowered than *some* male readers? Do these more privileged readers need to be "rescued"? Modleski seems to be as committed as her male counterpart, Robert Scholes, to saving feminism from the appropriative gestures of men (even well-intentioned ones): "feminist criticism performs an escape act dedicated to freeing women from *all* male captivity narratives, whether these be found in literature, criticism, or theory" (136). Though "Feminism and the Power of Interpretation" presents itself as a materialist investigation of "reading as woman," no allowance is made for the real, material differences between women. In the end, this materialist piece is curiously amaterialist in that the differences between women which would de-essentialize the category of Woman are treated, by their very omission, as *immaterial*.

The Essentialism in Anti-essentialism

All of this brings me to a possible way to negotiate the essentialist dilemma at the heart of these theories of "reading like a man"

(Scholes), "reading as a woman" (Culler), or reading like a "female feminist critic" (Modleski). It is by no means insignificant that nearly every piece in the volume *Men in Feminism*, of which Scholes's "Reading Like a Man" is one of the more noteworthy contributions, manifests a preoccupation with the question of place, specifically with the problem of where men stand in relation to feminism. Paul Smith wishes to claim for men the privileged space of displacement, usually reserved in deconstruction for Woman, in order to mark the difference of feminism, the subversive presence within. Stephen Heath speculates that the obsession with place is a male obsession with decidedly phallic overtones: are men "in" or "out" of feminism? Still others, Cary Nelson and Rosi Braidotti, suggest that men have no place (or at least no *secure* place) in feminism; according to this line of thinking, men may need feminism but feminism does not need men.[2] While place emerges as the recurrent theme that pulls together the twenty-four disparate essays which comprise *Men in Feminism*, I am also struck by how many of these articles inevitably come round to the question of essence, eventually invoke essentialism as the real impediment to theorizing men "in" feminism. An unarticulated relation between essence and place seems to motivate each piece. Certainly this book can be described as an investigation of the place of essence in contemporary critical discourse, but perhaps we should be interrogating not only the place of essentialism but the essentialism of place; one question might provide us with a gloss on the other. The remainder of this chapter will demonstrate that the essentialism in "anti-essentialism" inheres in the notion of place or positionality. What is *essential* to social constructionism is precisely this notion of "where I stand," of what has come to be called, appropriately enough, "subject-positions."

To understand the importance of place for social constructionist theory, we must look to Jacques Lacan's poststructuralist psychoanalysis. Lacan's return to Freud is, above all, a project which seeks to reclaim the place of subjectivity as a destabilizing and decentering force from the work of ego psychologists who, through their unquestioned allegiance to Western humanism, seek to re-encapsulate the subject within a stationary, traditional Cartesian framework. It is during the "pre-subject's" passage from the Imaginary into the Symbolic that the child, under the threat of castration, recognizes the different sexed subject-positions ("he," "she") and finally assumes one.[3] It is especially significant that throughout his work Lacan always speaks in terms of the *place* of the subject. His subversive rewriting of Descartes's "I think, therefore I am" (*cogito ergo sum*) as "I think where I am not, therefore I am where I do not think" provides a good case in point ("The Agency of the Letter in the Unconscious or Reason Since Freud" 1977, 166). The emphasis in Lacan's anti-cogito falls on the "where"; the question "who is speaking" can only be answered by shifting the grounds of the question to "where am I speaking from?" But it is important to remember that the place of the subject is nonetheless, ultimately, unlocalizable; were we able to fix the whereabouts of the subject in a static field of determinants, then we would be back in the realm of ego psychology. What is important about Lacan's emphasis on *place* is that thinking in terms of positionality works against the tendency of concepts such as "subject" and "ego," or "I" and "you," to solidify. The "I" in Lacanian psychoanalysis is always a precarious and unstable place to be—"intolerable," in fact, in one critic's estimation (Gallop 1985, 145).

Another recurrent emphasis in Lacan's work, useful for our purposes here, is his insistence on the *construction* of the subject's sexuality rather than the *de facto* assignation of a sex at birth. Lacan teaches us in "The Meaning of the Phallus" that we assume our sex, "take up its attributes only by means of a threat"—the threat of castration (Mitchell and Rose 1982, 75). It is because the birth of the subject does not coincide with the biological birth of the human person (Freud's fundamental insight into the problem of sexuality) that Lacan can speak in "The Mirror Stage" of "a real *specific prematurity of birth* in man" (1977, 4). Jane Gallop describes our delayed entry into subjectivity this way: "the child, although already born, does not become a self until the mirror stage. Both cases are two-part birth processes: once born into 'nature,' the second time into 'history' " (1985, 85). The "I," then, is not a given at birth but rather is constructed, assumed, taken on during the subject's problematic entry into the Symbolic. Lacan's focus on the complex psychoanalytic processes which participate in the constitution of the subject is, of course, a pre-eminently anti-essentialist position and, as we shall see, it has profound implications for the way in which we think about the subject who reads and the subject who is read.

I turn now to the theory of subject-positions most recently deployed, to brilliant effect, by Gayatri Spivak in her work on the subaltern. Spivak borrows and adapts her theoretical terminology not from Lacan but from Michel Foucault, although Lacan's theory of subjectivity is everywhere in the background here. It is in *The Archaeology of Knowledge* that Foucault elaborates his own notion of subject-positions as one of the four fundamental components of discursive formations. But before discussing the way in which "sub-ject-positions" can help us to read texts and to textualize readers, it is important to situate Spivak's turn to subjectivity in the context of her interest in the Subaltern Studies group, a Marxist historical collective devoted to the project of exposing and undermining the elitism which characterizes traditional approaches to South Asian culture.[4] Spivak's main critique of Subaltern Studies is, in fact, the classic critique generally leveled against materialists—namely, a failure to address adequately questions of subjectivity. Although deconstructivist in their goal to displace traditional historiography, the members of Subaltern Studies nevertheless rely on certain human-ist notions such as agency, totality, and presence. Spivak's "Subaltern Studies: Deconstructing Historiography" (1987, 197–221) is a sharp and discerning reading of the way in which the collective's entire attempt to "let the subaltern speak" falls prey to a positivistic search for a subaltern or peasant consciousness, which, in Spivak's opinion, can never be ultimately recovered.[5]

What is strikingly different about Spivak's reading of Subaltern Studies is that she does not dismiss their essentialism out of hand. In fact, she reads the collective's humanist ambitions to locate a subaltern consciousness as "a *strategic* use of positivist essentialism in a scrupu-lously visible political interest" (205). Wittingly or unwittingly, Subal-tern Studies *deploys* essentialism as a provisional gesture in order to align themselves with the very subjects who have been written out of conventional historiography:

> Although the group does not wittingly engage with the post-structur-alist understanding of "consciousness," our own transactional read-ing of them is enhanced if we see them as *strategically* adhering to the essentialist notion of consciousness, that would fall prey to an anti-humanist critique, within a historiographic practice that draws many of its strengths from that very critique. . . . If in translating bits and pieces of discourse theory and the critique of humanism back into an essentialist historiography the historian of subalternity aligns himself to the pattern of conduct of the subaltern himself, it is only a progressivist view, that diagnoses the subaltern as necessarily inferior, that will see such an alignment to be without interventionist value. Indeed it is in their very insistence upon the subaltern as the subject of history that the group acts out such a translating back, an interven-tionist strategy that is only partially unwitting. (206–207)

Spivak's simultaneous critique and *endorsement* of Subaltern Studies' essentialism suggests that humanism can be activated in the service of the subaltern; in other words, when put into practice by the dispossessed themselves, essentialism can be powerfully displacing and disruptive. This, to me, signals an exciting new way to rethink the problem of essentialism; it represents an approach which evaluates the motivations *behind* the deployment of essentialism rather than prematurely dismissing it as an unfortunate vestige of patriarchy (itself an essentialist category).

I do, however, have some serious reservations about treating essentialism as "a strategy for our times" (207). While I would agree with Spivak that a provisional return to essentialism can successfully operate, in particular contexts, as an interventionary strategy, I am also compelled to wonder at what point does this move cease to be provisional and become permanent? There is always a danger that the long-term effect of such a "temporary" intervention may, in fact, lead once again to a re-entrenchment of a more reactionary form of essentialism. Could it be that the recent calls, such as Spivak's, for a strategic essentialism might be humanism's way of keeping its fundamental tenets in circulation at any cost and under any guise? Could this be "phallocentrism's latest ruse"?[6] It may well be a ruse, but in the end I would agree that the "risk" is worth taking. I cannot help but think that the determining factor in deciding essentialism's political or strategic value is dependent upon who practices it: in the hands of a hegemonic group, essentialism can be employed as a powerful tool of ideological domination; in the hands of the subaltern, the use of humanism to mime (in the Irigarian sense of to undo by overdoing) humanism can represent a powerful displacing repetition. The question of the permissibility, if you will, of engaging in essentialism is therefore framed and determined by the subject-position from which one speaks.

We return, then, to Foucault's poststructuralist definition of "a subject" as "not the speaking consciousness, not the author of the formulation, but a position that may be filled in certain conditions by various individuals" (1972, 115). It is not difficult to translate Foucault's approach to subjectivity into a general theory of reading. For example, we might ask: what are the various positions a reading subject may occupy? How are these positions constructed? Are there possible distributions of subject-positions located in the text itself? Can a reader refuse to take up a subject-position the text constructs for him/her? Does the text construct the reading subject or does the reading subject construct the text? In "Imperialism and Sexual Difference," Spivak concludes that "the clearing of a subject-position in order to speak or write is unavoidable" (1986, 229). Now it is not clear exactly what Spivak means by this claim; is she referring to a clearing *away* of a previously held subject-position or a clearing the way *for* a particular subject-position? The ambiguity is instructive here, for when reading, speaking, or writing, we are always doing both at once. In reading, for instance, we bring (old) subject-positions to the text at the same time the actual process of reading constructs (new) subject-positions for us. Consequently, we are always engaged in a "double reading"—not in Naomi Schor's sense of the term,[7] but in the sense that we are continually caught within and between *at least* two constantly shifting subject-positions (old and new, constructed and constructing) and these positions may often stand in complete contradiction to each other.

Nothing intrinsic to the notion of subject-positions suggests that it may constitute a specifically *feminist* approach to reading; it is, however, especially compatible with recent feminist reconceptualizations of the subject as a site of multiple and heterogeneous differences. This work seeks to move beyond the self/other, "I"/"not-I" binarism central to Lacan's understanding of subject constitution and instead substitutes a notion of the "I" as a complicated field of multiple subjectivities and competing identities. There is some disagreement over whether or not this new view of the subject as heteronomous and heterogeneous marks a break with Lacan or represents the logical outcome of his theory. Teresa de Lauretis persuasively argues the former case:

> It seems to me that this notion of identity points to a more useful conception of the subject than the one proposed by neo-Freudian psychoanalysis and poststructuralist theories. For it is not the fragmented, or intermittent, identity of a subject constructed in division by language alone, an "I" continuously prefigured and preempted in an unchangeable symbolic order. It is neither, in short, the imaginary identity of the individualist, bourgeois subject, which is male and white; nor the "flickering" of the posthumanist Lacanian subject, which is too nearly white and at best (fe)male. What is emerging in feminist writings is, instead, . . . a subject that is not divided in, but rather at odds with, language. (1986, 9)

Mary Gentile, another feminist film critic, agrees, arguing that it is precisely women's "tentative" subjectivity (a result of their ambivalent representation as both object of desire and desire unfulfilled) which allows us to see subjectivity as a nexus of possibilities "where there is no clear split between 'I' and 'not-I,' but rather a range or continuum of existence" (1985, 19). My own position on the question is more closely aligned with Constance Penley's reasoning that the seeds of a theory of the subject as dispersed, as multiple, can already be found in

Lacan's notion of the subject as a place of contradiction, continually in a state of construction. This view holds that without Lacan's concept of the "split subject," divided against itself, these new feminist theories of identity would not be possible (1986, 145). In any case, what we can take away from this specific debate on Lacan's theory of subjectivity is, first, the strategy of positing the reader as a site of differences and, second, the notion of the reading process as a negotiation amongst discursive subject-positions which the reader, as social subject, may or may not choose to fill.

For Foucault, which subject-positions one is likely to read from is less a matter of "choice" than "assignation." Spivak's work clarifies for us that these "I-slots" are, in fact, institutional subject-positions— "social vacancies that are of course not filled in the same way by different individuals" ("A Literary Representation of the Subaltern" 1987, 304). Though it is always dangerous to speak in terms of "choice" within a poststructuralism which deconstructs such notions as agency and free will, Spivak still provides us with a modicum of movement between institutional subject-positions. Her own reading of Mahasweta Devi's "Breast-Giver" moves carefully and deliberately among the "I-slots" of author, reader, teacher, subaltern, and historian. I see two major difficulties in applying Foucault's notion of subject-positions to either a strategy or a theory of reading.[8] First, it leads to an inclination to taxonomize, to list one's various categorical positions in linear fashion as if they could be easily extracted and unproblematically distinguished from each other. Second, such a reading can easily lend itself to stereotyping, that is, to labeling "kinds" of readers and predicting their institutional responses as Tania Modleski does with her hypothetical male and female reader in "Feminism and the Power of Interpretation." Spivak seems to anticipate this objection when she rightly insists that "all generalizations made from subject-positions are untotalizable" (304); yet her discussions of "the Indian reader," "the Marxist-feminist reader," and especially "the non-Marxist anti-racist feminist readers in the Anglo-U.S." who, "for terminological convenience," she categorizes under the label "liberal feminism" (254) all seem to point to a totalizing picture supporting and upholding each "I-slot." Perhaps it is inevitable that we turn to such labels "for terminological convenience" (after all, how else are we to make any distinctions at all between readers?), yet the phone book compiling of "I-slot" listings can be unsettling if what we wish to emphasize is not the fixed differences between subject-positions but the fluid boundaries and continual commerce between them.

Still, there are a number of benefits to such a theory of reading based on the shifting grounds of subjectivity. First, the notion of subject-positions reintroduces the author into literary criticism without reactivating the intentional fallacy; the author's interpretation of his or her own text is recognized as a legitimate position among a set of possible positions a subject might occupy in relation to the text produced. Second, because subject-positions are multiple, shifting, and change-able, readers can occupy several "I-slots" *at the same time.* This dispersal suggests both that no reader is identical to him or herself and that no reading is without internal contradiction. Third, there is no "natural" way to read a text: ways of reading are historically specific and culturally variable, and reading positions are always constructed, assigned, or mapped. Fourth, basing a theory of reading on subjectivity undermines any notion of "essential readers." Readers, like texts, are constructed; they inhabit reading practices rather than create them *ex nihilo.* Finally, all of these points suggest that if we read from multiple subject-positions, the very act of reading becomes a force for dislocating our belief in stable subjects and essential meanings.

What is particularly surprising to me about the recent men in feminism debates is not the preoccupation with essence and place but the immobility, the intractableness of the privileged terms "men" and "feminism." Robert Scholes and Tania Modleski both work to *reinforce* the bar between men/feminism, each in effect erecting a defense against the incursions of the other. For although the goals of their critical projects are much the same, if not identical (to rescue feminism from the mastering impulses of deconstruction), these critics who are more allies than combatants nonetheless position themselves on opposite sides of the asymmetrical binarism: Scholes electing to read "like a man," and Modleski choosing to read like a "female feminist." Stephen Heath, on the other hand, has argued that "female feminism" can only be viewed as a contradiction in terms. Building on Elaine Showalter's influential "Critical Cross-Dressing: Male Feminists and the Woman of the Year," Heath concludes that a man reading as a feminist always involves a strategy of female impersonation ("Male Feminism," Jardine and Smith, 28). But is there not also a mode of impersonation involved when a woman reads as a feminist, or, indeed, when a woman reads as a woman? Heath tentatively suggests that "maybe the task of male critics is just to read (forget the 'as') . . ." (29), but Scholes is right to insist that we never "just" read, that we always read *from somewhere.* The anti-essentialist "where" is essential to the poststructuralist project of theorizing reading as a negotiation of socially constructed subject-positions. As its linguistic containment within the very term "displacement" might suggest, place can never be entirely displaced, as it were, from deconstruction.

Let me return, in conclusion, to the question I deferred at the beginning of this chapter: upon what grounds can we base the notion of a class of women reading? Both "class" and "women" are political constructs (a point I shall return to in the next chapter on Monique Wittig) but what, we might ask, is "politics"? Politics is precisely the self-evident category in feminist discourse—that which is most irreducible and most indispensable. As feminism's *essential* component, it tenaciously resists definition; it is both the most transparent and the most elusive of terms. The persistent problem for feminist theorists of locating a suitable grounds for a feminist politics finds perhaps its most urgent articulation in Donna Haraway's impressive work on "cyborg politics": "What kind of politics could embrace partial, contradictory, permanently unclosed constructions of personal and collective selves and still be faithful, effective?" (1985, 75). Her answer: a class of women linked together "through coalition—affinity, not identity"—affinity based on "choice" rather than on "nature" (73). My own inclination is to tackle these same questions of identity, politics, coalition, and feminism, but from the opposite direction. Whereas Haraway posits a coalition of women as the basis of a possible feminist socialist politics, I see politics as the basis of a possible coalition of women. For Haraway, it is affinity which grounds politics; for me, it is politics which grounds affinity. Politics marks the site where Haraway's project begins and where mine ends. In both cases, politics operates as the privileged, self-evident category.

The slippage in the above paragraph from "class" to "coalition" is not merely accidental. I intend to suggest by this shift an anti-essentialist reading of "class" as a *product* of coalition. Coalition precedes class and determines its limits and boundaries; we cannot identify a group of women until various social, historical, political coalitions construct the conditions and possibilities for membership. Many anti-essentialists fear that positing a political coalition of *women* risks presuming that there must first be a natural class of women; but this belief only masks the fact that it is coalition politics which constructs the category of women (and men) in the first place. Retaining the idea of women as a class, if anything, might help remind us that the sexual categories we work with are no more and no less than social constructions, subject-positions subject to change and to historical evolution. I am certainly not the first feminist to suggest that we need to retain the notion of women as a class for political purposes. I would, however, wish to take this conviction to its furthest conclusion and suggest that it is politics which feminism cannot do without, politics that is essential to feminism's many self-definitions. It is telling, I think, that constructionists are willing to displace "identity," "self," "experience," and virtually every other self-evident category *except* politics. To the extent that it is difficult to imagine a *non-political* feminism, politics emerges as feminism's essence.

3

Monique Wittig's
Anti-essentialist Materialism

The notion that traditional gender categories are historical or cultural productions and not natural or empirical givens is, as we have seen, pre-eminently a constructionist position. In recent years, anti-essentialists have carefully documented and rigorously critiqued those theories (both non-feminist and feminist alike) which seek to reduce the complex questions of sexual, racial, and even class differences to irreducible biological imperatives. Social constructionist feminists have brought under suspicion the idea of an irreducible, immutable, metaphysical essence defining "Woman" and have suggested instead that we can speak only of particular "women" constructed by variable and historically specific sets of social relations. It is my contention in this chapter that in our well-intentioned efforts to unmask and to denounce essentialism as a dangerous conceptual fallacy, we may have too quickly and perhaps too uncritically embraced constructionism as the necessary or only corrective. Constructionism is not quite the unproblematic, "safe" critical position we have so often taken it to be; indeed, constructionism creates certain methodological, epistemological, and political problems of its own, and these need to be discussed with the same vigor, intelligence, and healthy skepticism that feminists in the past have directed toward questions of essentialism. A consideration of some of the hitherto ignored problems with anti-essentialism necessarily entails a re-consideration of its theoretical Other, essentialism; if anti-essentialism is not entirely the secure philosophical position we have always presumed, then it may also be that essentialism fails to deliver as an infallible term of criticism and dismissal.

At present there remains a considerable amount of resistance to any calls such as this one for a reconsideration of essentialism's uses— strategic or otherwise; feminists have been "burned" in the past by those wishing to characterize women by an appeal to their essence, which, since Aristotle on, has been perceived as "naturally" inferior.

We need to continue to be rightly wary of such efforts by hegemonic groups to use essentialism as a political tool waged against less powerful groups. Still, it is precisely these powerless groups we need to listen to more carefully as we rethink the problem of essentialism in feminist theory, for it may well be that Gayatri Spivak is right: in the hands of the dispossessed themselves, essentialism can be a powerful strategic weapon. In order to delve more deeply into the complexity of these issues, I have elected to approach the essentialist/constructionist debate from two directions: the present chapter will focus on the theory of Monique Wittig, to plot out the "tension points" in her work between her materialism and her professed anti-essentialism, two positions which are not necessarily as compatible as they may at first seem; the following chapter will center on the work of another prominent French feminist, Luce Irigaray, and will explore the strategic motivations which underlie her theory of an essentialist psychoanalysis. The juxtaposition of these two chapters seeks to redress the critical imbalance between essentialism and constructionism, while my own position balances precariously between the two.

To begin, then, with Monique Wittig. Wittig is a French feminist materialist whose theoretical work is not perhaps as well known outside France as the work of some of her psychoanalytic colleagues (Hélène Cixous, Julia Kristeva, Luce Irigaray) but nor is it as prolific. I will be drawing, in eclectic if not irresponsible fashion, from six of Wittig's most important theoretical pieces published over the last decade: "Paradigm" (1979), "The Straight Mind" (1980), "One is Not Born a Woman" (1981), "The Category of Sex" (1982), "The Point of View: Universal or Particular?" (1983), and "The Mark of Gender" (1986). Each of these pieces elaborates a lesbian materialist approach to issues of language, culture, history, sexuality, and politics which grounds itself in a theory of constructionism, providing me with the opportunity to investigate some of the unposeable questions for an anti-essentialist materialist. In my efforts to disclose the hidden pitfalls often encountered in anti-essentialist discourse, I have chosen the work of Monique Wittig as my test case because it is Wittig who presents us with anti-essentialism in perhaps its strictest, most uncompromising form. I intend to demonstrate in what follows how anti-essentialism, when pushed to its extreme, risks collapsing into its opposite—essentialism; this critical conflation not only threatens the main enterprise of Wittig's work it also *enables* it, demonstrating in the end how anti-essentialism is always fundamentally dependent on essentialism in order to do its work.

"Lesbians are not women"

Wittig is perhaps best known for her formulation of the relationship between sex and oppression: sex, according to Wittig, does not create oppression; rather oppression creates sex:

> For there is no sex. There is but sex that is oppressed and sex that oppresses. It is oppression that creates sex and not the contrary. The contrary would be to say that sex creates oppression or to say that the cause (origin) of oppression is to be found in sex itself, in a natural division of the sexes preexisting (or outside of) society. (1982, 64)

For Wittig, nothing (including biology) exists before sociality; everything is socially constructed. What this means for the interpretation of sexual difference is that the categories "men" and "women" are political and not natural categories. "Difference" is merely itself a social construct—a product of a heterosexualizing discourse which Wittig calls "the straight mind": "the straight mind cannot conceive of a culture, a society where heterosexuality would not order not only all human relationships but also its very production of concepts and all the processes which escape consciousness as well" (1980, 107). Psychoanalysis, "the official discourse of sexuality" (1979, 114), represents to Wittig the most pervasive and most pernicious production of the straight mind; indeed, every discourse (but Wittig's own materialism it seems) falls prey to the straight mind's heterosexualizing operations and totalizing impulses. Wittig passionately attacks theorizations of the psyche which are "untouched by history and unworked by class conflicts" (1980, 104) and she has harsh words for some of her French feminist colleagues who, in her opinion, buy into the apolitical, ahistorical projects of psychoanalysis and subsequently fail to account for the real material and economic oppression of women. Throughout the corpus of her work, Wittig insists on the materiality of women's oppression and the power of discourses to inflict violence and to further domination. As she forcefully puts it in "The Straight Mind": "there is nothing abstract about the power that sciences and theories have, to act materially and actually upon our bodies and our minds, even if the discourse that produces it is abstract" (106).

What I have tried to do all too briefly here is to summarize some central themes and concepts which occur with regularity in Wittig's theoretical texts. Wittig is first and foremost a materialist thinker who believes that nothing which signifies can "escape the political in this moment in history" (1980, 105) and who further maintains that what is most politically urgent at this particular historical moment is nothing less than the destruction of the categories of sex, the abolition of women as a materially oppressed class, and the institution of a new epistemology to subvert and to supplant "the straight mind." How can these three related goals be achieved? For Wittig, the answer lies in her definition of "lesbian" and in its radically subversive location in a heterosexual culture. The false dichotomy between heterosexual and homosexual, which Wittig believes circumscribes and subtends phallocentric economies, is fractured and disseminated through this third term, lesbian. It is the lesbian who demonstrates, by her very existence, that women are not a natural group or an essential category, for, in patriarchal culture, lesbians are labeled "not real women" thereby disclosing the act of social construction implicit in the very naming of "women."[1]

Let me analyze for a moment Wittig's theorization of "lesbian"—at once her most provocative and her most problematical concept. In one of the more startling articulations in "The Straight Mind," Wittig pronounces that indeed "lesbians are not women," but in a different sense than intended by the homophobic versions of this same claim:

> It would be incorrect to say that lesbians associate, make love, live with women, for "women" has meaning only in heterosexual systems of thought and heterosexual economic systems. Lesbians are not women. (110)

Or, in "One is Not Born a Woman," she explains that lesbians are not women because women are defined strictly by their relation of dependency on men, and lesbians, in their sexual practices at least, escape this relation of domination altogether:

> Lesbian is the only concept I know of which is beyond the categories of sex (woman and man), because the designated subject (lesbian) is *not* a woman, either economically, or politically, or ideologically. For what makes a woman is a specific social relation to a man, a relation that we have previously called servitude. (53)

A lesbian, then, is a not-woman and a not-man; she is blatantly a cultural construction and obviously not a product of nature. The strength of this analysis is Wittig's strong constructionist perspective, her persistent unmasking of the biologist, naturalist discourses frequently underlying discussions of the body and of sexual difference.

The weakness of her analysis lies in her own tendency to homogenize lesbians into a single harmonious group and to erase the real material and ideological differences between lesbians—in other words, to engage in essentialist thinking in the very act of trying to discredit it.

Wittig's essentializing gestures are perhaps most obvious in her scattered comments on "lesbian culture." In "Paradigm" we learn that lesbianism is a separate culture, "an international culture with its own literature, its own painting, music, codes of language, codes of social relations, codes of dress, its own mode of work" (117). We might add to this list of features "its own sexuality," for Wittig sees lesbianism as constituting a free cultural space—free of violence, free of control, even free of social determination:

> For us sexuality has only a distant relation with heterosexuality, since the latter is dominated by its final cause, reproduction, and since the obligatory exercise of heterosexuality, far from having as its goal the sexual expansion of individuals, assures an absolute control of their physical persons. (1979, 118)

Significantly, while the categories of sex, which are for Wittig essentializing constructions of domination and mystification, must be destroyed, the category "lesbian" remains intact: "to destroy 'woman,' does not mean that we aim, short of physical destruction, to destroy lesbianism simultaneously with the categories of sex, because lesbianism provides for the moment the only social form in which we can live freely" (1981, 53). One might question whether, as a social construction, lesbianism is not also somehow "obligatory" or "learned," rather than freely chosen. Can there be such a thing as "free space" in a strict anti-essentialist view, and how might such a reliance on the humanist notions of freedom, self-determination, and individualism undermine Wittig's social constructionist project?

Surely, what Wittig ought to be talking about is not lesbian culture, but lesbian *cultures*, not "the lesbian body" (the title of one of her best-known novels) but *lesbian bodies*, not lesbian sexuality but *lesbian sexualities*. "Lesbian" is itself an unstable, changing, and historically specific category which all too often becomes reified and solidified in Wittig's theoretical texts. Phrases such as "that is the point of view of a lesbian" (1983, 64) or "a lesbian subject as the absolute subject" (1986, 72) are troubling because, in or out of their textual contexts, they suggest that a lesbian is innocent and whole, outside history, outside ideology, and outside change. To return to Lacanian psychoanalysis for a moment, Wittig's "lesbian" functions as a transcendental signifier, occupying none other than the place of the Lacanian phallus. This is undoubtedly a bold move, but occupying the place of transcendental signifier also subjects "lesbian" to all its attendant limitations, most especially a certain ideality of the sign. One implication of this ideality is that Wittig's theory is unable to account for heterosexual feminists except to see them as victims of false consciousness. Adrienne Rich has attempted to resolve this particular problem in "Compulsory Heterosexuality and Lesbian Existence" by positing a "lesbian continuum" which covers "a wide range—through each woman's life and throughout history—of woman-identified experience" (1983, 192). Rich's declaration of identity in "Split at the Root: An Essay on Jewish Identity"—"I am a woman; I am a lesbian" (1986, 103)—transgresses the Wittigian divide between lesbian and woman by collapsing the apparent differences between them. We can therefore counter Wittig's controversial assertion that "lesbians are not women" with Rich's equally arguable claim that "all women are lesbians." But neither of these definitional statements seems entirely adequate. If Wittig is unable to account for the specificity of women who do not identify as lesbian, Rich (quite paradoxically) is unable to account for the specificity of those women who *are* lesbians. Whereas Wittig's notion of "lesbian" is too exclusive, too reified, Rich's notion is too inclusive, too vague. Both definitions are inspiring and creative, but they are also ahistorical and amaterialist—too imprecise to be useful epistemologically, though enormously evocative politically.

The lack of consensus and the continued disputes amongst feminists over the definition of "lesbian" pivot centrally around the question of essentialism. Exactly who is a lesbian? Is there such a thing as a lesbian essence? Does "woman" include "lesbian"? Can we speak of a "lesbian mind" as distinct from what Wittig calls "the straight mind"? The definitions of lesbian in feminist discourse are various and inventive. As a counterweight to Rich's overly general "lesbian continuum," Catharine Stimpson provides us with an admittedly "conservative and severely literal" definition of lesbianism as "a commitment of skin, blood, breast, and bone" (1982, 244). Audre Lorde offers a more metaphysical definition of lesbians as "strongly women-identified women where love between women is open and possible, beyond physical in every way" (Hammond 1980, 18). To Judy Grahn, "the subject of lesbianism/is very ordinary; it's the question/of male domination/that makes everybody/angry" (1978, 55). Bonnie Zimmerman attempts to pull together the metaphysical with the severely literal by positing a lesbian essence which must nonetheless be consistently and continuously historicized: "I do believe that there is a common structure—a lesbian 'essence,' " she confesses, but "careful attention to history teaches us that differences are as significant as similarities" (1985, 215–16). My own position is that "lesbian" is a historical construction of comparatively recent date, and that there is no eternal lesbian essence outside the frame of cultural change and historical determination. Such a view accords with the recent invention theories of homosexuality which I will discuss in greater detail in Chapter Six. Suffice it to say here that we need constantly to guard against the temptation to deconstruct "man" and "woman" as essential categories while reconstructing "lesbian" as a pure space above and beyond the problematics of sexual difference.

The Place of Male Homosexuality in Lesbian-Feminist Theory

Wittig's construction of "lesbian" as an unchanging, ahistorical, natural category poses one instance where we can see how essentialism inheres in anti-essentialism and threatens to undo the hierarchical relation between them. In the remainder of this chapter, I will locate in Wittig's work other symptomatic moments, other points of contradiction, where the text—in a self-deconstructing articulation—differs from itself and activates a displacement of the essentialist/constructionist opposition. These instances in which Wittig's constructionist discourse conflates into essentialism demonstrate that constructionism is itself a fluid and unstable category, a constantly shifting and often contradictory position. A second essentializing moment in Wittig which deserves our attention can be found in her treatment of male homosexuality. In "Paradigm" Wittig, presumably in an allusion to Greek antiquity, interprets male homosexuality as a phenomenon "quite often considered with the greatest respect." Why? "Because the fascination that masters exercise on masters is justified and even logical, for how a master can be fascinated by, and desire a slave is not very clear" (120). David Halperin has recently argued that for the Athenian adult male citizen the sexual act was a gesture of *sociopolitical* domination; his desire was targeted for his social inferiors (boys, women, slaves, and foreigners) and not his social equals, as Wittig suggests here (see Halperin 1986). But whether we agree with Wittig or not, it unfortunately leads her to dismiss, in preemptory fashion, the homophobia, hatred, and violence so often directed against gay men in this culture. Eve Sedgwick's distinction between "homosocial" and "homosexual" strikes me as a useful one here (see Sedgwick 1985), for while social relations between men may in many cultures be held in high regard, sexual relations between men are most often stigmatized and vilified.

A year later, in "The Straight Mind," Wittig poses her own corrective to this problem by resituating gay men in the category of the dominated other, rather than the dominating subject:

> For heterosexual society is the society which not only oppresses lesbians and gay men, it oppresses many different/others, it oppresses all women and many categories of men, all those who are in the position of the dominated. (108)

In Wittig's early work, gay men alternately assume the variable positions of oppressor and oppressed, victimizer and victimized, subject and object: as homosexuals, they are oppressed (by straight women for example); as men, they are oppressing; as gay men, they are, to borrow a line from Luce Irigaray, "both at once." Now, given the dual position of gay men in society, it would seem that male homosexuals pose the truly subversive category in a heterosexual culture for they collapse the hierarchy of self and other by fulfilling both roles simultaneously; this transgression of boundaries throws into question the essentialist view of men as always and everywhere dominating and women as always and everywhere dominated. But we have arrived at a point directly antithetical to the ostensible goal of Wittig's entire project which is to position lesbianism, and not male homosexuality, as her privileged third term, the very category that has the power to reverse and to displace the heterosexual/homosexual polarity which constitutes the straight mind. I believe that in Wittig's work, male homosexuality comes to function as a repressed other, a subversive category that threatens the stability of her privileged trope "lesbian" at the same time that it performs the vital (though unacknowledged) function of preventing it from solidifying. Wittig's stated aim in both "Paradigm" and "The Straight Mind" is to replace "homosexual" as a category with "lesbian" as a category because the homosexual/heterosexual binarism is a product of the straight mind. But with this strategic move, gay men drop out of focus altogether, and indeed, if we examine the texts which follow "The Straight Mind," male homosexuality has been wholly and completely elided. It may well be that Wittig is leaving open the possibility for a male subject, "gay" or "straight," to fill the category "lesbian," but this intriguing line of inquiry is not, unfortunately, pursued. Instead, a new binarism has been constructed, this time a split between lesbians and male homosexuals, with the second term subordinated to and obscured by the first.

Much lesbian-feminist theory sets up the lesbian subject as a natural agent of subversion, an inherent revolutionary subject. According to

Adrienne Rich, simply by virtue of being a lesbian a woman occupies a privileged if embattled space of cultural resistance: "Lesbian existence comprises both the breaking of a taboo and the rejection of a compulsory way of life. It is also a direct or indirect attack on male right of access to women. . . . We may first begin to perceive it as a form of nay-saying to patriarchy, an act of resistance" (1983, 192). It is puzzling that gay men are not accorded the same revolutionary status as lesbians in either Wittig's or Rich's theories of sexual politics; given the way in which gay men, in their social and sexual practices, radically challenge the current notions of masculinity and the "naturalness" of heterosexual desire, one would think that they, too, disrupt and disable the logic of the straight mind (or what Rich prefers to call the "institution of compulsory heterosexuality"). But Adrienne Rich's landmark essay in the still nascent field of lesbian-feminist theory, "Compulsory Heterosexuality and Lesbian Existence," is curiously unable to theorize male homosexuality outside of its popular negative stereotypes.

Rich focuses on the "qualitative differences" between gay male relations and lesbian relations, "for example, the prevalence of anonymous sex and the justification of pederasty among male homosexuals, the pronounced ageism in male homosexual standards of sexual attractiveness, and so forth" (193). She wishes to "move toward a dissociation of lesbian from male homosexual values and allegiances" (193) believing that male homosexuality is centrally implicated in the interests and abuses of patriarchy. Thus, "the issue of 'lesbian sadomasochism' needs to be examined in terms of the dominant cultures' teachings about the relation of sex and violence, and also of the acceptance by some lesbians of male homosexual mores" (203). It is telling that Rich sees lesbian s/m as, in effect, a false or perverted form of lesbian sex: practitioners of lesbian s/m have been either duped by "the dominant cultures' teachings" or influenced by "male homosexual mores." The unfortunate corollary of this position is the insinuation that some forms of lesbianism are truer than others. It is also important to note here that Rich, through the lever of her "lesbian continuum," would rather ally lesbian and heterosexual women against the institution of patriarchy than ally lesbians and gay men against the institution of compulsory heterosexuality. Gay men are seen to be acting out the "values" of a patriarchal society through their involvement in unequal power relations (pederasty) and through their susceptibility to "ageism" and "anonymous sex." Lesbians, in contrast, if they do succumb to such "values" participate out of false consciousness— against their "true nature" as monogamous, faithful, mutually loving sexual beings.

The real problem with both Wittig's theory of "the straight mind" and Rich's theory of "compulsory heterosexuality" is the assumption that heterosexuality is as natural and beneficial for men as it is unnatural and destructive for women. We do not have to look far to locate the roots of this problem in object-relations theory. Nancy Chodorow's theory of *The Reproduction of Mothering* (1978) is at this point well known, but a skeletal summary of her basic thesis might highlight some of the crucial gaps in the object-relations argument which allow male homosexuality to slip through the theoretical machinery. According to Chodorow, both sexes are parented by a woman. Both sexes long for a return to the primary union with the female, a return to the pre-oedipal state of oneness with the maternal body. But whereas a man can directly reproduce the exclusive mother-child relationship through the heterosexual bond, a woman cannot simulate the lost primordial oneness with the maternal through heterosexual intercourse, and so she chooses to recreate this primal unity by herself becoming a mother. This in many ways intriguing theory of the reproduction of mothering cannot, however, satisfactorily account for the reproduction of *heterosexuality*. Though everything in Chodorow's work points specifically towards a theory of female homosexuality, lesbianism is virtually dismissed with the preemptive opinion that "lesbian relationships do tend to recreate mother-daughter emotions and connections, but most women are heterosexual" (200).[2] Rich is quite right when she indicts Chodorow's theory of mothering as less a critique of compulsory heterosexuality than a mandate for it. Rich does not, however, challenge Chodorow's fundamental theory that the object of all desire is first *and last* for women; such a theory cannot account for male homosexuality except to read it as a perversion. The total absence of any discussion of male homosexuality in Chodorow's book is no mere oversight but rather (if I may be permitted to trope on Luce Irigaray) "the blind spot of an old dream of maternity." I cannot help but feel that the critical aporia upon which object-relations theories such as Chodorow's depend is the enigmatic difference of male homosexuality; a man's sexual desire for a woman is natural, a figurative and literal return to the female body; a woman's sexual desire for a man is psychically strained (a displacement of her primary love for other women) but a necessary means of recuperating the maternal by herself becoming a mother; a woman's sexual desire for another woman is perhaps *more* natural than desire for a man, but, for inadequately explained historical reasons, it is also "rare"; a man's sexual desire for a man is, well, simply inexplicable.

To Luce Irigaray, the repression of male homosexuality in Western culture is not so inexplicable since the deferral of actual male homosexual relations simply functions as a veil for the "hom(m)o-sexual monopoly," a monopoly which structures the economy around the exchange of women: "reigning everywhere, although prohibited in practice, hom(m)o-sexuality is played out through the bodies of women, matter, or sign, and heterosexuality has been up to now just an alibi for the smooth workings of man's relations with himself, of relations among men" (*This Sex*, 172). But here again, real homosexual men drop out of the analysis.[3] For Irigaray, the very foundations of patriarchal culture are based upon the exchange of women between men; in the sexual and economic marketplace, "there are producer subjects and agents of exchange (male) on the one hand, productive earth and commodities (female) on the other" (*This Sex*, 192). What this theory of a phallically organized economy does not recognize is that there is more than one market, that there are as many systems of commodification and exchange as there are sets of social relations. A subject can be located in several economies, in competing and perhaps even incompatible social orders, at the same time. There seems little reason to assume that a theory of hom(m)o-sexuality must be predicated on a single market of exchange, a separate and universal system of commerce. Moreover, even if we agree that there is a single, global market, a gay man can still be interpellated simultaneously as an agent who exchanges (a "producer subject") and a body that is exchanged (a "commodity object"): as a man he can reap all the benefits of a patriarchal system; as a *gay* man, seen to occupy the powerless, feminized position of exchange, he is denied many of the benefits which accrue to heterosexuals in a heterosexist culture. To insist on the plurality and unpredictability of sexual economies, then, may open a space in lesbian-feminist theory for a more adequate theorization of male homosexuality and, concomitantly, a less romanticized theorization of lesbianism.

The Matter of Biology

A third moment where we can locate essentialist underpinnings to an anti-essentialist argument is Wittig's theorization of the body and its place in materialist discourse. Wittig is caught in a paradox: on the one hand, as a materialist, she insists that we deal with the real, material oppression of women and the domination of women's anatomical bodies; on the other hand, as an anti-essentialist, she seeks to abolish the category of sex and the notion that men and women constitute natural, anatomical groups. Materialist feminist ideology destroys the idea of men and women "considered as materially specific in their bodies" (1981, 47), but it also insists that we address "the material oppression of individuals by discourses" as it plays itself out on the specific bodies of women (1980, 106). In truth, "the body" is itself a cultural construction for Wittig and she is hesitant to discuss the body outside the context of what she calls "social reality" (1980, 106). But such a strict social constructionist position may risk throwing the baby out with the bathwater. As Denise Riley puts it, " 'biologism' as a dismissive category ignores the fact that there really is biology" (1984, 2). Anti-essentialist materialists run the risk of too quickly dismissing both biology and psychology as essentializing discourses, often failing to recognize the irreducible essentialism informing their own theorizations.

Rosalind Coward asks: "how is it that a society unilaterally affects anatomical women in one way, and anatomical men in another way? And what is it about that anatomical state which guarantees that anatomical men and women will consistently take up these roles, as social men and women?" (1983, 267). This is a question which poses something of a theoretical stumbling block for anti-essentialists. Coward has demonstrated how the social constructionist argument, which holds that we are made not born, though superficially an anti-essentialist position still contains within it a core or residue of essentialism: a notion of anatomical raw material culturally shaped and conditioned. But a strict anti-essentialist might respond by arguing that there is no raw material upon which social mechanisms operate. As a materialist, Wittig states unequivocally that nothing exists prior to or outside matter (1981, 51), yet, as an anti-essentialist, she also suggests that the body is not matter—at least in any pure or natural sense—but rather is a pure social construction. Obviously what we need to say here, as Wittig does, is that matter is itself socially constructed. But one can talk about the body as matter, it seems to me, without presuming that matter has an essence. Most anti-essentialists, however, are hesitant to discuss the body at all for fear of sounding essentializing. This caution leads Wittig, in the end, to elide the material body almost completely, and she achieves this lacuna by effecting a nearly imperceptible slippage from the formulation "the body *is* not matter" to the position "the body *does* not matter": *it matters not*. What is lost in her work is precisely a materialist analysis of the body *as* matter.

The same problem emerges in Christine Delphy's *Close to Home: A Materialist Analysis of Women's Oppression* (1984). Delphy, a cofounder with Wittig of the radical feminist journal *Questions fémi-nistes*, subscribes to the same rigorous anti-essentialist premises we have already seen in Wittig: "it is *oppression which creates gender*," she writes, echoing Wittig in "The Category of Sex"; "*gender, in its turn created anatomical sex*" (144). Delphy's work makes explicit what Wittig's theory merely implies—namely, that biology (the anatomical, material body) does not deserve our serious theoretical attention:

> Feminists have been shouting for at least twelve years, and still shout, whenever they hear it said that the subordination of women is caused by the inferiority of our natural capacities. But, at the same time, the vast majority continue to think that 'we musn't ignore biology'. But why not exactly? (23)

To Delphy, "the role that biology never merited historically it does not merit logically either" (23). What feminists therefore need to do, in this view, is not merely to resist collapsing sex with gender (the biologi-cal with the social) but to erase the category of sex altogether:

> One of the axioms, if not the fundamental axiom, of my approach is that women and men are *social* groups. I start from the incontestable fact that they are socially named, socially differentiated, and socially pertinent, and I seek to understand these social practices. How are they realized? What are they for? It may be (and again this remains to be proven) that women are (also) females, and that men are (also) males, but it is women and men that interest me, not females and males. (24)

What Delphy is objecting to, specifically, is the way in which sex supersedes and occludes gender, the way in which, through their mere association, sex inevitably *naturalizes* gender.

Delphy's insistence on the primacy of the social and the political, and on the dangers of positing natural explanations for sociopolitical effects, are notions fundamental to constructionist theory, and it is not my goal here to undercut a position to which I myself so strongly subscribe. On the contrary, my intention is to buttress the social con-structionist position by suggesting that substituting social determinism for biological determinism, and replacing sex with gender, may not be the most productive ways to deal with the question of biology. Biology will not simply go away, much as we might wish it to; it has to be theorized. It seems to me crucial that, rather than bracket "females and males" (that is, erase the category of sex), we might learn more by interrogating the relations between female and woman, woman and women, women and feminist. It is precisely by taking on what Elizabeth Weed has called the impossible "relation of women to Woman" ("A Man's Place," in Jardine and Smith 1987, 74) that we might avoid what Wittig and Delphy both warn against: the essentialist gesture of automatically reading "men" and "women" as metaphysical categories. Such an approach would encourage us to push the social constructionist analysis further and to pose the more urgent questions: what is the natural? the biological? the social? the cultural? How is the body acted upon by the social? How is the social articulated by the body?[4]

In "Notes Toward a Politics of Location," Adrienne Rich makes the timely suggestion that "perhaps we need a moratorium on saying 'the body.' " The distinction Rich constructs between *the* body and *my* body strikes me as a useful place to begin the project of reintroducing biology, the body *as matter*, back into poststructuralist materialist discourse:

> it's also possible to abstract 'the body.' When I write 'the body,' I see nothing in particular. To write 'my body' plunges me into lived experience, particularity: I see scars, disfigurements, discolorations, damages, losses, as well as what pleases me. . . . To say 'the body' lifts me away from what has given me a primary perspective. To say 'my body' reduces the temptation to grandiose assertions. (1986, 215)

The body connotes the abstract, the categorical, the generic, the scientific, the unlocalizable, the metaphysical; *my* body connotes the particular, the empirical, the local, the self-referential, the immediate, the material. The simultaneous nearness and distance between the definite article "the" and the personal pronoun "my" carries all the weight and tension of the essentialist/constructionist antagonism, for whereas the determiner "the" essentializes its object through universalization, the possessive "my" de-essentializes its object through particularization. A politics of location, such as Rich proposes, must begin both from "the geography closest in—the body" (212), and from the effort "to locate myself in my body" (215). The difficult but necessary mediation between "the" and "my" also brings us back to the centrality of subject-ositions, to "recognizing our location, having to name the ground we're coming from" (219); such a naming cannot ignore the role social practices play in organizing and imaging "the body," but nor can it overlook the role "my body" plays in the constitution of subjectivity.

The critical aporia in much anti-essentialist theory on the subject of the body's materiality must be confronted and in some way accounted for if we are to negotiate successfully the current stand-off between essentialists and constructionists. Of course, not *all* feminist poststructuralists jettison the anatomical body from the field of their investigations. Luce Irigaray has engaged the female body head on in her controversial theories of *parler femme* and the two lips. Predictably, such fearlessness toward speaking the body has earned for Irigaray the dismissive label "essentialist." But as I now hope to demonstrate, Irigaray speaks a language of essence which participates in the very construction and symbolization of the female body; hers is an essentialism profoundly intricated with the grammar and logic of social constructionism.

4

Luce Irigaray's
Language of Essence

In the preceding chapter, I attempted to demonstrate how, in the work of at least one French feminist materialist, Monique Wittig, anti-essentialism is made both possible and impossible, at once tenable and tentative, by the essentialist moments upon which it elaborates its own system. In the present chapter, I turn to the work of Luce Irigaray, a French psychoanalyst and philosopher, a "psychophilosophical" writer in Carolyn Burke's words (1981, 289), in order to deconstruct the essentialist/constructionist binarism "from the other side"—the side of essentialism and, in this instance, of psychoanalysis. If essentialism symptomatically inheres in anti-essentialist formulations, is it possible that essentialism may itself be predicated, in turn, on some mode of anti-essentialism? Does essentialism, when pushed to *its* extreme, collapse into anti-essentialism? What might be at stake in deploying essentialism for strategic purposes? In short, are there ways to think and to talk about essence that might not, necessarily, "always already," *ipso facto*, be reactionary?

In what follows it will become clear that I do believe that there are such ways to elaborate and to work with a notion of essence that is not, *in essence*, ahistorical, apolitical, empiricist, or simply reductive. But before turning to a consideration of Irigaray's strategic use of essentialism, it bears emphasizing that most of the criticisms leveled against Irigaray's work since the publication of *Speculum de l'autre femme* in 1974 are inevitably based upon or in some way linked to this fear of essentialism. A summary sample of the most important and oft-cited of these criticisms is enough to demonstrate how impassioned and genuine the resistance to essentialism is for many feminists, and how problematic the reassessment of essentialism's theoretical or political usefulness is likely to be.

Irigaray and Her Critics

In 1981, two critical essays on Luce Irigaray's work were published in the U.S., each in a well-known feminist academic journal: Christine Fauré's "The Twilight of the Goddesses, or the Intellectual Crisis of French Feminism" appeared in *Signs*, and Carolyn Burke's "Irigaray Through the Looking Glass" appeared in *Feminist Studies*. Fauré's critique, a translation from the French, is unquestionably the more severe. She objects to a general trend in French feminist theory, epitomized by Irigaray's search for a female imaginary, which marks "a retreat into aesthetics where the thrust of feminist struggle is masked by the old naturalistic ideal draped in the trappings of supposedly 'feminine' lyricism" (1981, 81).[1] Carolyn Burke also wonders whether Irigaray's work escapes the very idealism which her deconstruction of selected philosophical and psychoanalytic texts so rigorously and persistently seeks to displace:

> Does her writing manage to avoid the construction of another idealism to replace the 'phallogocentric' systems that she dismantles? Do her representations of a *parler femme*, in analogy with female sexuality, avoid the centralizing idealism with which she taxes Western conceptual systems? (1981, 302)

Metaphysical idealism is perhaps the most damaging of the many criticisms charged against Irigaray; it finds its most recent and perhaps most powerful rearticulation in Toril Moi's *Sexual/Textual Politics*:

> Any attempt to formulate a general theory of femininity will be metaphysical. This is precisely Irigaray's dilemma: having shown that so far femininity has been produced exclusively in relation to the logic of the Same, she falls for the temptation to produce her own positive theory of femininity. But . . . to define 'woman' is necessarily to essentialize her. (1985, 139)

Is it true that any definition of "woman" must be predicated on essence? And does Irigaray, in fact, define "woman"? Though I will later argue that the problem of an idealism based on the body, on an essential femininity, is fundamentally a misreading of Irigaray, suffice it to say here that Moi's assumption that "to define 'woman' is necessarily to essentialize her" is by no means self-evident.

While Irigaray has been criticized by both psychoanalysts and materialists alike, the most impassioned critiques have come primarily from the materialists. Monique Plaza's "'Phallomorphic Power' and the Psychology of 'Woman,' " first published in the French radical feminist publication *Questions féministes* and later reprinted in the British Marxist journal *Ideology and Consciousness*, offers the most sustained and unremittingly critical indictment of Irigaray's apparent essentialism. According to Plaza, Luce Irigaray's great mistake (second only to her general failure to interrogate adequately psychoanalytic discourse) is a tendency to confuse social and anatomical categories; Irigaray's theorization of female pleasure and her "search for the feminine 'interior' " lead her to abjure the category of the social and to practice a dangerous form of "pan-sexualism which is only a coarse, disguised naturalism" (1978, 8 and 9). Plaza, along with Monique Wittig and Christine Delphy, argues from the materialist standpoint that "nature" is always a product of social relations and that sex is always a construction of oppression and never its cause. It is the move to desocialize "woman," Plaza insists, which leads Irigaray into the fallacy of essentialism:

> The absence of a theory of oppression, the belief in the unavoidable and irreducible sexual Difference, the psychologistic reduction, the inflation of the notion of "woman" which one finds in Luce Irigaray's investigation, can only result in this essentialist quest. In the gap left by the statement of woman's non-existence, Luce Irigaray will set up a "new" conception of woman. (28)

Plaza goes on to accuse Irigaray of positivism, empiricism, and negativism (31). Toril Moi, another materialist critic, adds two more weighty epithets: ahistoricism and apoliticism (1985, 147–48). If this were a critical barbecue, Irigaray would surely be skewered.

Luce Irigaray, however, is not without her defenders. Jane Gallop, in "Quand nos lèvres s'écrivent: Irigaray's Body Politic," interprets Irigaray's persistent focus on the female labia as a *construction* rather than a *reflection* of the body; Irigaray's essentialism is thus read within a larger constructionist project of re-creating, re-metaphorizing the body (1983, 77–83). Margaret Whitford takes a similarly sympathetic (which is not to say uncritical) approach to the question of essentialism in Irigaray's work. In "Luce Irigaray and the Female Imaginary: Speaking as a Woman," Whitford concludes that while Irigaray does sometimes blur the distinctions between the social and the biological, "this is obviously a strategy adopted within a particular historical and cultural situation" (1986, 7).[2] This particular response to the problem of essentialism in Irigaray strikes me as the most promising line of argument to follow, for rather than foreclosing the discussion on essentialism before it has truly begun, this approach asks the more difficult question: if Irigaray appeals to a mode of feminine specificity, and if (unlike Wittig) she attempts to speak the female body, what might such strategic forays into the territory of essentialism allow her to accomplish? What might Irigaray's work amount to *if she refused* such admittedly risky ventures into "this sex which is not one"?

"By our lips we are women"

Let me begin to answer these questions by re-examining the place and function of the "two lips" in Irigaray's theorization of female pleasure. This concept is perhaps most responsible for generating the charges of essentialism. Three words neatly summarize for Irigaray the significance of the two lips: "Both at once." Both at once signifies that a woman is simultaneously singular and double; she is "already two— but not divisible into one(s)," or, put another way, she is *"neither one nor two"* (*This Sex*, 24, 26). It is the two lips which situate women's autoeroticism, their pleasure, in a different economy from the phallic, in an economy of ceaseless exchange and constant flux:

> Woman's autoeroticism is very different from man's. In order to touch himself, man needs an instrument: his hand, a woman's body, language . . . And this self-caressing requires at least a minimum of activity. As for woman, she touches herself in and of herself without any need for mediation, and before there is any way to distinguish activity from passivity. Woman "touches herself" all the time, and moreover no one can forbid her to do so, for her genitals are formed of two lips in continuous contact. Thus, within herself, she is already two—but not divisible into one(s)—that caress each other. (*This Sex*, 24)

It would be hard to deny, on the basis of this particular passage, that Irigaray proposes to give us an account of female pleasure based on the body's genitalia; and it would be hard to deny that her account of the phallus is any less morphological.[3] Why the essentialist language here? Why the relentless emphasis on the two lips?

Let me turn first to the Irigarian critique of the phallus to demonstrate what appears to be a strategic misreading of male genitalia. According to Irigaray, Western culture privileges a mechanics of solids over a mechanics of fluids because man's sexual imaginary is isomorphic; as such, the male imaginary emphasizes the following features: "production, property (proprieté), order, form, unity, visibility, erection" (1985, 77). The features associated with a female imaginary, as we might expect, more closely approximate the properties of liquids: "continuous, compressible, dilatable, viscous, conductible, diffusable" (*This Sex*, 111). The problem here is simply that many of the properties Irigaray associates with the two lips might also describe the penis. As K.K. Ruthven points out:

> A good deal depends here on the accuracy of Irigaray's characterization of the penis as "one" in comparison with the "not one" of the vulva. Certainly, her theory seems to require the penis to be always inflexibly erect and quite without metamorphic variation, and also to be circumcised, as the presence of a foreskin endows it with most of the properties she attributes to the labia. (1984, 100–101)

Irigaray's reading of phallomorphism as a kind of isomorphism, however, is not so much a misreading as an *exposure* of one of the dominant metaphors in poststructuralist psychoanalysis. It is not Irigaray who erects the phallus as a single transcendental signifier but Lacan: Irigaray's production of an apparently essentializing notion of female sexuality functions strategically as a reversal and a displacement of Lacan's phallomorphism.

Irigaray's critique of Lacan centers primarily on his refusal to listen to women speak of their own pleasure; she finds most untenable Lacan's insistence that, on the subject of pleasure, women have nothing to say. In his Seminar XX on women, Lacan listens not to women but to art, not to Saint Theresa but to Bernini's statue of Saint Theresa: "you only have to go and look at Bernini's statue in Rome to understand immediately that she's coming, there is no doubt about it" ("God and the *Jouissance* of The Woman," in Mitchell and Rose 1982, 147). Irigaray's interrogatory response in "Così Fan Tutti" deftly unmasks the phallocentrism at play here: "In Rome? So far away? To look? At a statue? Of a saint? Sculpted by a man? What pleasure are we talking about? Whose pleasure?" (*This Sex*, 90–91). Her logic is irrefutable: why would a woman need to go all the way to Rome to discover the "truth" of her pleasure? Why, after all, is "the right to experience pleasure . . . awarded to a statue" (*This Sex*, 90)?

Irigaray's "When Our Lips Speak Together" provides an explanatory gloss on Lacan's efforts to arrive at the truth of woman's pleasure through an appeal to a statue: "Truth is necessary for those who are so distanced from their body that they have forgotten it. But their truth immobilizes us, turns us into statues . . ." (*This Sex*, 214). If women are turned into statues through the process of specularization—through the agency of the look—how can this specular economy be undone? How, in other words, can women begin to speak their own pleasure? Throughout both *Speculum of the Other Woman* and *This Sex Which Is Not One*, Irigaray supplants the logic of the gaze with the logic of touch: it is the "contact of *at least two* (lips) which keeps woman in touch with herself but without any possibility of distinguishing what is touching from what is touched" (*This Sex*, 26). This shift of focus from sight to touch affords Irigaray another opportunity to challenge Lacan, this time on the subject of his obsession with veiling: "Veiling and unveiling: isn't that what interests them? What keeps them busy? Always repeating the same operation, every time. On every woman" (*This Sex*, 210). A woman's exchange of herself with herself, without the agency of the literal penis or the Symbolic phallus, is exactly what puts into question the prevailing phallocratic and specular economy.

It is tempting to compare Wittig's concept of "lesbian" and Irigaray's notion of the "two lips," since both work to rethink the place and status of the phallus in Western culture. For Wittig, "lesbian" operates as a new transcendental signifier to replace the phallus; it is outside the system of exchange and keeps the system open. Irigaray's "two lips," while also outside of a phallic economy, do not function in the same way, since the lips articulate a female imaginary and not a cultural symbolic. Still, it is not always easy to distinguish the imaginary from the symbolic in Irigaray, especially since the female imaginary is repeatedly theorized in relation to the symbolic agencies of language and speech. Margaret Whitford comes closest to pinpointing Irigaray's departure from Lacan; in the Irigarian account of female sexuality, "what is needed is for the female imaginary to accede to its own specific symbolisation" (1986, 4).

This symbolization of the female imaginary is precisely what Irigaray seeks to elaborate through her conceptualization of the two lips. The sustained focus in her work on this particular trope operates in at least two ways. First, it has the desired effect of historically foregrounding "the more or less exclusive—and highly anxious—attention paid to erection in Western sexuality" and it demonstrates "to what extent the imaginary that governs it is foreign to the feminine" (*This Sex*, 24). Second, it poses a possible way out of one of the most troubling binds created for feminist psychoanalysts: the problem of how to acknowledge the formative role of the Symbolic, the arm of phallocracy, while still subscribing to the notion of feminine specificity. To turn once again to that lyrical love letter, "When Our Lips Speak Together," Irigaray's testing of the essentialist waters becomes total submersion: "no event makes us women," she explains, rather "by our lips we are women" (*This Sex*, 211, 209–10). Unlike Wittig, who severs the classification "woman" from any anatomical determinants, there can be little doubt that, for Irigaray, a woman is classified as such on the basis of anatomy:

> Your/my body doesn't acquire its sex through an operation. Through the action of some power, function, or organ. Without any intervention or special manipulation, you are a woman already. (*This Sex*, 211)

The point, for Irigaray, of defining women from an essentialist standpoint is not to imprison women within their bodies but to rescue them from enculturating definitions by men. An essentialist definition of "woman" implies that there will always remain some part of "woman" which resists masculine imprinting and socialization:

> How can I say it? That we are women from the start. That we don't have to be turned into women by them, labeled by them, made holy and profane by them. That has always already happened, without their efforts. . . . It's not that we have a territory of our own; but their fatherland, family, home, discourse, imprison us in enclosed spaces where we cannot keep on moving, living, as ourselves. Their properties are our exile. (*This Sex*, 212)

To claim that "we are women from the start" has this advantage—a political advantage perhaps pre-eminently—that a woman will never be a woman solely in masculine terms, never be wholly and permanently annihilated in a masculine order.

"Rolled up in metaphors"

Perhaps what most disturbs Irigaray's critics is the way in which the figure of the two lips becomes the basis for theorizing a speaking (as) woman, a *parler femme*. Many American feminists are disturbed by the French feminist tendency to link language and the body in any way, literally or metaphorically. It bothers Elaine Showalter, for example, that "while feminist criticism rejects the attribution of literal biological inferiority, some theorists seem to have accepted the *metaphorical* implications of female biological difference in writing." Showalter believes that "simply to invoke anatomy risks a return to the crude essentialism, the phallic and ovarian theories of art, that oppressed women in the past" (1982, 17). Mary Jacobus concurs, arguing that "if anatomy is not destiny, still less can it be language" (1982, 37), and Nancy K. Miller similarly insists in her criticism of the French feminists that a "woman-text" must be sought in "the body of her writing and not the writing of her body" (1980, 271). It is interesting to note, as Jane Gallop does, that all the critics included in *Writing and Sexual Difference* (a volume which includes Showalter's "Feminist Criticism in the Wilderness" and Jacobus's "The Question of Language: Men of Maxims and *The Mill on the Floss*") have difficulty accepting the metaphoricity of the body; they demand that metaphors of the body be read literally, and they then reject these metaphors as essentialistic (Abel 1982, 802).[4]

The debate over Irigaray's essentialism inevitably comes down to this question of whether the body stands in a literal or a figurative relation to language and discourse: are the two lips a metaphor or not? What I propose to argue here is that, for Irigaray, the relation between language and the body is neither literal nor metaphoric but *metonymic*. Though Irigaray disparages what she calls the " 'masculine' games of tropes and tropisms" (*Speculum*, 140), she is not without her own favorite tropes, chief among them the figure of metonymy. But before examining the way in which Irigaray deconstructs the predominance of metaphoricity in Western culture and creates a space for metonymy, a brief consideration of what Irigaray actually says about speaking (as) woman is in order.

Irigaray's project is to explore the "distinction of the sexes in terms of the way they inhabit or are inhabited by language" (*This Sex*, 100); her work represents "an attempt to define the characteristics of what a differently sexualized language would be" (1985, 84). This line of inquiry leads her to ask how women can "already speak (as) women." Her answer? "By going back through the dominant discourse. By interrogating men's 'mastery.' By speaking to women. And among women" (*This Sex*, 119). The chapter entitled "Questions" in *This Sex Which Is Not One* provides us with a series of clarifications on what a speaking (as) woman might be and how it can be put into practice:

> Speaking (as) woman . . . implies a different mode of articulation between masculine and feminine desire and language. (*This Sex*, 136)

> Speaking (as) woman is not speaking of woman. It is not a matter of producing a discourse of which woman would be the object, or the subject. (*This Sex*, 135)

> There may be a speaking-among-women that is still a speaking (as) man but that may also be the place where a speaking (as) woman may dare to express itself. (*This Sex*, 135)

> Speaking (as) woman would, among other things, permit women to speak *to* men. (*This Sex*, 136)

> It is certain that with women-among-themselves . . . something of a speaking (as) woman is heard. This accounts for the desire or the necessity of sexual nonintegration: the dominant language is so powerful that women do not dare to speak (as) woman outside the context of nonintegration. (*This Sex*, 135)

Parler femme appears to be defined not so much by what one says, or even by how one says it, but from whence and to whom one speaks. Locus and audience distinguish a speaking (as) woman from a speaking (as) man: "by *speaking (as) woman*, one may attempt to provide a place for the 'other' as feminine" (*This Sex*, 135). Is it only *from* this "place" that women can speak to women, or is it precisely by speaking *to* women that the speaker can achieve a *parler femme?* Irigaray's response would be "both at once" since for a woman to speak she must establish a locus from which to be heard, and to articulate such a space, she must speak.

Closely connected to the notion of *parler femme* is Irigaray's conception of two syntaxes (one masculine, one feminine) which cannot accurately be described by the number "two" since "they are not susceptible to comparison" (*Speculum*, 139). These syntaxes are "irreducible in their strangeness and eccentricity one to the other. Coming out of different times, places, logics, 'representations,' and economies" (*Speculum*, 139). The two syntaxes cannot be compared since the relation between them is not based on similarity but contiguity, in other words, not on metaphor but on metonymy. Like the "two lips," they "touch upon" but never wholly absorb each other. Contiguity, it turns out, operates as the dominant feature of a *parler femme*, the distinguishing characteristic of a feminine syntax:

> what a feminine syntax might be is not simple nor easy to state, because in that "syntax" there would no longer be either subject or object, "oneness" would no longer be privileged, there would no longer be proper meanings, proper names, "proper" attributes . . . Instead, that "syntax" would involve nearness, proximity, but in such an extreme form that it would preclude any distinction of identities, any establishment of ownership, thus any form of appropriation. (*This Sex*, 134)

Impacted within this list of what a feminine syntax is *not*—subject, object, oneness, appropriation, and so on—a positive description emerges: nearness and proximity. We return to the figure of the two lips as a model for a new kind of exchange:

> Ownership and property are doubtless quite foreign to the feminine. At least sexually. But not *nearness*. Nearness so pronounced that it makes all discrimination of identity, and thus all forms of property, impossible. Woman derives pleasure from what is *so near that she cannot have it, nor have herself*. She herself enters into a ceaseless exchange of herself with the other without any possibility of identifying either. This puts into question all prevailing economies. . . . (*This Sex*, 31)

To speak (as) woman is ceaselessly to embrace words and persistently to cast them off. To touch upon but never to solidify, to put into play but never to arrive at a final telos or meaning, isn't this another way to speak about "différance"? Carolyn Burke seems to think so when she proposes that Irigaray offers us a "vaginal" fable of signification to supplement, but not replace, Derrida's "hymeneal" fable (1981, 293 and 303). I don't believe, however, that Irigaray would ever use such a term or endorse such a concept as "vaginal fable" since it limits female pleasure to a single erogenous zone by overprivileging the vagina and denying that a woman's sexuality is plural: in fact, "a woman's erogenous zones are not the clitoris or the vagina, but the clitoris and the vagina, and the lips, and the vulva, and the mouth of the uterus, and the uterus itself, and the breasts . . ." (*This Sex*, 63–4). The sites of woman's pleasure are so diffuse that Irigaray wonders whether the qualifier "genital" is still even required (*This Sex*, 64).

If the trope of nearness does not function in the way Burke suggests, as yet another non-synonymic term for "différance,"[5] it does appear to facilitate a deconstruction of the metaphor/metonymy binarism operative in Western philosophical discourse. Roman Jakobson defines these two polar figures of speech in "Two Aspects of Language and Two Types of Aphasic Disturbances," a study of speech disorders in which he demonstrates that all varieties of aphasia can be identified as an impairment either of the faculty for "selection and substitution" (metaphor) or of the faculty for "combination and contexture" (metonymy). Metaphor operates along the axis of similarity whereas metonymy operates along the axis of contiguity (Jakobson and Halle 1956, 76).[6] In theories of language metaphor has long dominated over metonymy.[7] We see this dominance played out in Lacanian psychoanalysis where the phallus stands in a privileged metaphoric relation to the body (it "stands for" sexual difference), and where the "paternal metaphor" emerges as the privileged signifier. Why is metaphor validated over metonymy? Exactly what role does the paternal metaphor play in Lacan's theorization of sexual difference and its construction? Jacqueline Rose identifies three symbolic functions:

> First, as a reference to the act of substitution (substitution is the very law of metaphoric operation), whereby the prohibition of the father takes up the place originally figured by the absence of the mother. Secondly, as a reference to the status of paternity itself which can only ever logically be inferred. And thirdly, as part of an insistence that the father stands for a place and a function which is not reducible to the presence or absence of the real father as such. (Mitchell and Rose 1982, 38–39)

Rose goes on to defend Lacan against the charge of phallocentrism, arguing that we must recognize that for Lacan "the status of the phallus is a fraud" (because castration is a fraud) and so we must not literalize the phallus and reduce it to the level of the penis (40 and 45).

While this line of argument is compelling enough, and certainly faithful to Lacan's own conception of the phallus, still the contiguity between the penis and the phallus, the *proximity* and *nearness* of these two terms, gives one pause. Mary Ann Doane puts the problem this way:

> Does the phallus really have nothing to do with the penis, no commerce with it at all? The ease of the description by means of which the boy situates himself in the mode of "having" one would seem to indicate that this is not the case. . . . There is a sense in which all attempts to deny the relation between the phallus and the penis are feints, veils, illusions. The phallus, as signifier, may no longer *be* the penis, but any effort to conceptualize its function is inseparable from an imaging of the body. (1981, 27–28)[8]

The problem, put another way, is simply that the relation between the penis and the phallus is as much one of association or metonymy as similarity or metaphor. The same might be said of Irigaray's treatment of the "two lips," the only difference being that Irigaray allocates the metonymic function to the two lips and relegates metaphor to the realm of Lacan's phallomorphism.

Irigaray has this to say about a woman's historical relation to meta-phoricity: a woman is "stifled beneath all those eulogistic or denigra-tory metaphors" (*Speculum*, 142–43); she is "hemmed in, cathected by tropes" (*Speculum*, 143) and "rolled up in metaphors" (*Speculum*, 144). One wonders to what extent it is truly possible to think of the "two lips" as something *other* than a metaphor. I would argue that, despite Irigaray's protestations to the contrary, the figure of the "two lips" never stops functioning metaphorically. Her insistence that the two lips escape metaphoricity provides us with a particularly clear example of what Paul de Man identifies as the inevitability of "reenter-ing a system of tropes at the very moment we claim to escape from it" (1984, 72). But, what is important about Irigaray's conception of this particular figure is that the "two lips" operate as a metaphor *for* metonymy; through this collapse of boundaries, Irigaray gestures to-ward the deconstruction of the classic metaphor/metonymy binarism. In fact, her work persistently attempts to effect a historical displace-ment of metaphor's dominance over metonymy; she "impugns the privilege granted to metaphor (a quasi solid) over metonymy (which is much more closely allied to fluids)" (*This Sex*, 110). If Freud was not able to resist the seduction of an analogy,[9] Irigaray insists that no analogy, no metaphoric operation, completes her:

> Are we alike? If you like. It's a little abstract. I don't quite understand 'alike.' Do you? Alike in whose eyes? in what terms? by what stan-dard? with reference to what third? I'm touching you, that's quite enough to let me know that you are my body. (*This Sex*, 208)

Lacan writes that the play of both displacement and condensation (metaphor and metonymy) mark a subject's relation to the signifier; they operate, in fact, as the laws which govern the unconscious. A question oft-repeated in Irigaray is "whether the feminine *has* an un-conscious or whether it *is* the unconscious" (*This Sex*, 73). Is it possible that the feminine neither has an unconscious of its own nor represents man's unconscious but rather articulates itself as a specific operation within the unconscious: the play of metonymy?

A Politics of Essence

Irigaray's favorite topics—the two lips, *parler femme*, a feminine syntax, an economy of fluids—all seem to suggest that she is more interested in questions of subjectivity, desire, and the unconscious than in questions of power, history, and politics. In one sense, this is true;

as a "psychophilosopher," Irigaray places greater emphasis on the
"psychical" than on the "social." However, her work is not entirely
without what one might call a certain political perspicacity. Monique
Plaza, Beverly Brown, Parveen Adams, and Ann Rosalind Jones all
question whether a psychoanalytic investigation of the feminine can
adequately account for women's social oppression. As Jones puts it,

> feminists may still doubt the efficacy of privileging changes in subjec-
> tivity over changes in economic and political systems; is this not
> dangling a semiotic carrot in front of a mare still harnessed into
> phallocentric social practices? (Jones 1985, 107)[10]

Plaza goes further and indicts Irigaray for providing not a theory of
oppression but an oppressive theory (1978, 24–25). While I think it is
true that Irigaray does not provide us with a blueprint for social action,
I also find her work politically aware and even practically useful. Any
discussion of Irigaray's "politics of essence" must begin with her own
understanding of politics and, specifically, with her comments on what
a feminist politics might be.

Irigaray's explicit remarks on political practice, the women's movement in France (the MLF), and women's social oppression are largely
concentrated in the selection from her interviews, seminar remarks,
and conversations published under the title "Questions" in *This Sex
Which Is Not One*. It seems that readers and students of Irigaray most
want her to talk about the political significance of her work, its impact
on social practice, and its relation to current political activism in
France, perhaps because *Speculum* appears, on the surface, to jettison
so completely the category of the political in favor of the philosophical
and psychoanalytic. Irigaray seems eager to respond to her critics. If
Plaza and others see her work as reactionary because it is apolitical,
Irigaray is likely to respond that they are working with too limited or
rigid a notion of politics, that they are perhaps thinking only in terms
of a masculine politics:

> Strictly speaking, political practice, at least currently, is masculine
> through and through. In order for women to be able to make them-
> selves heard, a 'radical' evolution in our way of conceptualizing and
> managing the political realm is required. (*This Sex*, 127)

For Irigaray, politics—a "feminine" politics—is inseparable from the
project of putting the feminine into history, into discourse, and into
culture. Because of the contingent, future condition of this latter proj-

ect, Irigaray acknowledges that in fact "we cannot speak . . . of a feminine politics, but only of certain conditions under which it may be possible" (*This Sex,* 128).

The nascent condition of a *feminine* politics, however, does not preclude discussion of a *feminist* politics. "Liberation" (loosely understood by Irigaray as the introduction of the feminine into practice) is not an "individual" task:

> A long history has put all women in the same sexual, social, and cultural condition. Whatever inequalities may exist among women, they all undergo, even without clearly realizing it, the same oppression, the same exploitation of their body, the same denial of their desire. That is why it is important for women to be able to join together, and to join together "among themselves". . . . The first issue facing liberation movements is that of making each woman "conscious" of the fact that what she has felt in her personal experience is a condition shared by all women, thus *allowing that experience to be politicized.* (*This Sex,* 164)

A different notion of politics does seem to emerge here—a politics based not so much on group militancy or open confrontation as on shared "experience." But this notion of politics sounds suspiciously like the popular approved method of politicization in the early years of the Women's Movement in both France and America: consciousness-raising. And as such, it is subject to many of the same criticisms— especially the charge by numerous "marginal" feminists that what white, heterosexual, middle-class, and educated women feel in their personal experience does *not* necessarily represent "a condition shared by all women." Irigaray might rightly be accused here of a certain tendency to universalize and to homogenize, to subsume all women under the category of "Woman." Still, her work is not always insensitive to the axes of difference which divide "women-among-themselves." Consider:

> I think the most important thing to do is to expose the exploitation common to all women and to find the struggles that are appropriate for each woman, right where she is, depending upon her nationality, her job, her social class, her sexual experience, that is, upon the form of oppression that is for her the most immediately unbearable. (*This Sex,* 166–67)

Here we see the typical Irigarian double gesture: Irigaray proposes a feminist politics that will work on two fronts at once—on one side, a "global" politics that seeks to address the problem of women's universal oppression, and on the other side, a "local" politics that will address the specificity and complexity of each woman's particular situation. In order to accomplish "both at once," Irigaray believes that "it is essential for women among themselves to invent new modes of organization, new forms of struggle, new challenges" (*This Sex,* 166). The phrase "women-among-themselves" suggests a call for separatism, and indeed Irigaray does, cautiously, endorse separatism as a valid political strategy for feminists:

> For women to undertake tactical strikes, to keep themselves apart from men long enough to learn to defend their desire, especially through speech, to discover the love of other women while sheltered from men's imperious choices that put them in the position of rival commodities, to forge for themselves a social status that compels recognition, to earn their living in order to escape from the condition of prostitute . . . these are certainly indispensable stages in their escape from their proletarization on the exchange market. But if their aim were simply to reduce the order of things, even supposing this to be possible, history would repeat itself in the long run, would revert to sameness: to phallocratism. (*This Sex,* 33)

Irigaray believes that separatism can be a legitimate *means* to escape from a phallic economy but not an adequate goal; she sees it as a *tactical option* rather than a final telos. Above all, she does not want to foreclose the possibility that the politics of women-among-themselves might itself be a way to put the feminine into practice.

Through her comments on what a feminist politics might be, Irigaray broadens the notion of politics to include psychic resistance. She does not rule out direct political activism; she simply insists that resistance must operate on many levels:

> women must of course continue to struggle for equal wages and social rights against discrimination in employment and education, and so forth. But that is not enough: women merely "equal" to men would be "like them," therefore not women. (*This Sex,* 165–66)

Irigaray seems to imply here that women both already have an identity on which to base a politics and that they are striving to secure an identity through the practice of politics. In either case, the concept of "identity" has long been a problem for feminist poststructuralists seeking to base a politics on something other than "essence." Is it possible to generate a theory of feminine specificity that is not essentialist? How do we reconcile the poststructuralist project to displace identity with the feminist project to reclaim it? For Irigaray the solution is again double: women are engaged in the process of both constructing and deconstructing their identities, their *essences,* simultaneously.[11]

This "double gesture" towards essentialism is mirrored in the attempt of at least one of Irigaray's defenders to make sense of her complicated theorization of identity. In a clearly sympathetic reading of Irigaray's construction of feminine specificity, Paul Smith seems unable to make up his mind on the question of whether Irigaray is or is not an essentialist. On the one hand, he persuades us that "Irigaray's aim is . . . not quite to claim a privileged essence for women's 'two lips' but to propose a radically different construct (or a radical construct of difference)." On the other hand, Smith upholds Irigaray's essentialism as an exemplary "moment of contestation" (1988, 144), the very model for the kind of political resistance his book *Discerning the Subject* so persistently and urgently calls for. Smith in fact adds his own voice to the growing chorus of theorists demanding a judicious reassessment of essentialism's political efficacy:

> the charge of essentialism—common as it is—does not necessarily or always amount to the damning criticism it is supposed to be. Within the logic of feminism's still evolving constitution essentialist claims are perhaps becoming more and more important. (144)

But despite his endorsement of essentialism as a legitimate tactical device for feminists to deploy when necessary, Smith nonetheless is reluctant to place Irigaray entirely in the essentialist camp. His final say on the matter is quite striking for the ambiguity of its articulation and for the strategy that may lie behind such a tentative and ultimately guarded reading of Irigaray's theorization of the body: "Irigaray's reference to the female body is finally not to be understood as essentialist *in any familiar way*" (emphasis mine, 145). Is Smith suggesting that Irigaray is not at all an essentialist, or that she is indeed an essentialist but of a very particular kind? What Smith might mean exactly by a "familiar essentialism" is nowhere clarified in his reading of feminism's various accounts of the "subject," but this is not to say that such an approach is unhelpful or obfuscating. On the contrary, Smith's defense of Irigaray is no less persuasive for its vacillations and ambiguities; such apparent analytical caginess on the subject of Irigaray's essentialism works so well precisely because Irigaray both *is and is not* an essentialist; to sound a by now familiar theme, she is "both at once."

The process of laying claim to "essence" at first appears to be a politically reactionary maneuver; but one needs to place Irigaray's essentialism in the larger historical context of Western philosophy in order to comprehend how she might be using it strategically. In Aristotelian philosophy, "woman" has a very specific relation to essence, distinct from "man's" relation to essence. Only man properly *has* an essence; subjecthood is attained as he strives, in Irigaray's words, "to realize his essence as perfectly as he can, to give full expression to his *telos*" (*Speculum,* 164).[12] Because only subjects have access to essence, "woman" remains in unrealized potentiality; she never achieves "the wholeness of her form"—or if she has a form, it is merely "privation" (*Speculum,* 165). Woman is the ground of essence, its precondition in man, without herself having any access to it; she is the ground of subjecthood, but not herself a subject:

> Is she unnecessary in and of herself, but essential as the non-subjective sub-jectum? As that which can never achieve the status of subject, at least for/by herself. Is she the indispensable condition whereby the living entity retains and maintains and perfects himself in his self-likeness? (*Speculum,* 165)

In a phallocratic order, woman can never be more than "the passage that serves to transform the inessential whims of a still sensible and material nature into universal will" (*Speculum,* 225).

Irigaray's reading of Aristotle's understanding of essence reminds me of Lacan's distinction between *being* and *having* the phallus: a woman does not *possess* the phallus, she *is* the Phallus.[13] Similarly, we can say that, in Aristotelian logic, a woman does not *have* an essence, she *is* Essence. Therefore to give "woman" an essence is to undo Western phallomorphism and to offer women entry into subjecthood. Moreover, because in this Western ontology existence is predicated on essence, it has been possible for someone like Lacan to conclude, *remaining fully within traditional metaphysics,* that without essence, "woman does not exist." Does this not cast a rather different light on Irigaray's theorization of a woman's essence? A woman who lays claim to an essence of her own undoes the conventional binarisms of essence/accident, form/matter, and actuality/potentiality. In this specific historical context, to essentialize "woman" can be a politically strategic gesture of displacement.

To say that "woman" does not have an essence but *is* Essence, and at the same time to say that she has no access herself to Essence as Form, seems blatantly contradictory. Moreover, has not Western philosophy always posited an essence for woman—an essence based on biology and, as everyone knows, defined by the properties of weakness, passivity, receptivity, and emotion, to name just a few? The problem, I would argue, is not with Irigaray; it is precisely Irigaray's deployment of essentialism which clarifies for us the contradiction at the heart of Aristotle's metaphysics. In his philosophy, we see that the figure of "woman" has become the site of this contradiction: on the one hand, woman is asserted to have an essence which defines her as woman and yet, on the other hand, woman is relegated to the status of matter and can have no access to essence (the most she can do is to facilitate man's actualizing of his inner potential). I would go so far as to say that the dominant line of patriarchal thought since Aristotle is built on this central contradiction: woman has an essence and it is matter; or, put slightly differently, it is the essence of woman to have no essence. To the extent that Irigaray reopens the question of essence and woman's access to it, essentialism represents not a trap she falls into but rather a key strategy she puts into play, not a dangerous oversight but rather a lever of displacement.

What, then, constitutes woman's essence? Irigaray never actually tells us; at most she only approximates—"touches upon"—possible descriptions, such as the metonymic figure of the two lips. In fact, she insists that "woman" can never be incorporated in any theory, defined by any metaphysics. "What I want," Irigaray writes, "is not to create a theory of woman, but to secure a place for the feminine within sexual difference" (*This Sex*, 159). Elsewhere she explains that "for the elaboration of a theory of woman, men, I think, suffice. In a woman('s) language, the concept as such would have no place" (*This Sex*, 123). Irigaray works towards securing a woman's access to an essence of her own, without actually prescribing what that essence might be, or without precluding the possibility that a subject might possess multiple essences which may even contradict or compete with one another. Thus Irigaray sees the question "Are you a woman?" to be precisely the wrong question. Let me conclude with her playful challenge to all those who would press her to define the essence of "woman": "'I' am not 'I,' I *am* not, I am not *one*. As for *woman*, try and find out . . ." (*This Sex*, 120).

5

"Race" Under Erasure?
Poststructuralist
Afro-American Literary Theory

In his 1901 autobiography *Up From Slavery,* Booker T. Washington tells a most remarkable story. Sitting in the Jim Crow section of the train, on one of his many fund-raising trips for Tuskegee, Washington witnessed the following scene which, given this speech-maker's flair for telling an anecdote, I here cite in full:

> There was a man who was well known in his community as a Negro, but who was so white that even an expert would have hard work to classify him as a black man. This man was riding in the part of the train set aside for the coloured passengers. When the train conductor reached him, he showed at once that he was perplexed. If the man was a Negro, the conductor did not want to send him into the white people's coach; at the same time, if he was a white man, the conductor did not want to insult him by asking him if he was a Negro. The official looked him over carefully, examining his hair, eyes, nose, and hands, but still seemed puzzled. Finally, to solve the difficulty, he stooped over and peeped at the man's feet. When I saw the conductor examining the feet of the man in question, I said to myself, "That will settle it"; and so it did, for the trainman promptly decided that the passenger was a Negro, and let him remain where he was. I congratulated myself that my race was fortunate in not losing one of its members.

"How difficult it sometimes is to know where the black begins and the white ends," Washington muses (82). The story poses some rather difficult questions along these lines. Is "race" a question of morphology, of anatomical or genetic characteristics—such as the shape of the feet? If "race" is not a biological feature, then what kind of attribute or category is it: psychological, historical, anthropological, sociological, legal . . . ? Is race a matter of birth? of culture? both? neither? What, exactly, are the criteria for racial identity? *Are* there criteria for racial identity? What, we might finally ask, is "race"?

Critics of Afro-American literature have been profoundly interested of late in these questions on race; in fact, the deconstruction of "race" and its implications for reading literature by or about Afro-American subjects has emerged as one of the most controversial questions in the field of Afro-American Studies today. In an attempt to map out the various shifting positions of a complex and politically volatile debate, this chapter will range widely over four principal texts: *Black Literature and Literary Theory* (1984), *"Race," Writing, and Difference* (1986) (both volumes under the editorship of Henry Louis Gates, Jr.), Houston A. Baker, Jr.'s *Blues, Ideology, and Afro-American Literature: A Vernacular Theory* (1984), and the exchange in *New Literary History* between Gates, Baker, and Joyce A. Joyce on "The Black Canon: Reconstructing Black American Literary Criticism" (Winter 1987).[1] Primary attention will be devoted to the recent work of Anthony Appiah, Henry Louis Gates, Jr., and Houston A. Baker, Jr., three scholars at the center of the current debates on "race." I will begin, however, not with an African philosopher nor with an Afro-American literary critic but with a French Antillean psychiatrist, Frantz Fanon; Fanon's study of the Antillean subject under colonialism—a study part philosophy, part sociology, part literary criticism, part politics, and part psychoanalysis—offers a useful way of tracing the many arbitrary significations of "race."

Signifying "Race"

In fact, Frantz Fanon's *Black Skin, White Masks* (1952) provides us with something of a running commentary on the arbitrariness of the racial signifier in Western culture. Fanon begins with its codings in language, "race" as the product and the property of linguistic mastery: "To speak a language is to take on a world, a culture. The Antilles Negro who wants to be white will be the whiter as he gains greater mastery of the cultural tool that language is" (38). To speak a language, then, entails more than the assumption of "a world, a culture"; it presumes the acquisition of "a race." Mastery of the French language affords the Antillean access to whiteness—"honorary citizenship," as Fanon puts it (38)—in the same way that the Afro-American's suppression of black dialect and mastery of standard (white) English operates as a cultural bleaching process intended to produce a new product, complete with the nationalist tag "made in the U.S.A."

In a chapter aptly titled "The Fact of Blackness," Fanon addresses the biological signification of race in a culture where it is always the Other who is designated as ethnic, always the Other who assumes the badge and the burden of "race." It is not merely that to be a "Negro" in the French Antilles is to possess a particular genetic or biological make-up; it is, rather, to *be* the biological. Fanon links white fear of black bodies—what he calls "Negrophobia" and what we ordinarily call "racism"—to the colonialist inscription of the black African as primitive and sub-human—an animal located somewhere on the chain of being between man and ape (and presumably closer to the latter): "To suffer from a phobia of Negroes is to be afraid of the biological. For the Negro is only biological. The Negroes are animals. They go about naked" (165). Fanon calls this white representation of the black subject's extreme otherness "the image of the biological-sexual-sensual-genital-nigger" (202). It is important to remember that Fanon composed *Black Skin, White Masks* at a time when scientists still believed they could invent a serum for "denegrification" (111), a serum that would release unfortunate blacks from the prison of their bodies by chemically whitening those bodies from within. For Fanon, the body image of the black subject is not constituted by biological determinations from within but rather by cultural overdeterminations from without: "not only must the black man be black," Fanon writes, "he must be black in relation to the white man" (110). As Fanon sees it, his job as a psychoanalyst must be geared towards assisting his Antillean patients in abandoning their attempts at a "hallucinatory whitening" (100).

Fanon identifies racial signifiers in categories other than the most common, the linguistic and the biological; for example, additional codings of "race" addressed in *Black Skin, White Masks* are the symbolic ("In Europe, the black man is the symbol of evil," 188), the economic ("one is white above a certain financial level," 44), and the moral ("he is Negro who is immoral. If I order my life like that of a moral man, I simply am not a Negro," 192).[2] But perhaps we need look no further than Fanon's title, *Black Skin, White Masks,* to ascertain the author's own approach to signifying "race." The title is suggestive: it foregrounds the possibility of culturally assuming racial identities ("white masks") at the same time it underscores the priority and ineradicability of the racial body ("black skin"). The gap, marked by the comma, between "Black Skin" and "White Masks" allows simultaneously for an essentialist and a constructionist reading; it unhinges "race" from skin color at the same time it reinscribes the problematic association of race with biology. So where does Fanon arrive at the end of his tropological investigation? He arrives at this enigmatic destination: "The Negro is not. Any more than the white man" (231).

Is Fanon suggesting, perhaps, that there is no such thing as race? If so, his conclusions anticipate recent scholarship in the sciences that suggest that "race" is indeed a fiction with no empirical or scientific basis for its existence. Anthony Appiah, an analytic philosopher, articulates the scientific point of view in his controversial article, "The Uncompleted Argument: Du Bois and the Illusion of Race":

> Contemporary biologists are not agreed on the question of whether there are any human races, despite the widespread scientific consensus on the underlying genetics. . . . Every reputable biologist will agree that human genetic variability between the populations of Africa or Europe or Asia is not much greater than that within those populations. . . . Apart from the visible morphological characteristics of skin, hair, and bone, by which we are inclined to assign people to the broadest racial categories—black, white, yellow—there are few genetic characteristics to be found in the population of England that are not found in similar proportions in Zaire or in China; and few too (though more) which are found in Zaire but not in similar proportions in China or in England. (1985, 21–22)[3]

One recognizes in this argument the traces of a deconstructive operation (the difference *between* populations is not much greater than the difference *within* populations)[4] which allows the scientist or the philosopher to question the status of "race" as a valid empirical category. Following Appiah's lead, literary critic Henry Louis Gates, Jr. also maintains that "race" is an arbitrary signifier without any true referential moorings; it operates merely as a fiction or a trope—albeit a profoundly powerful one:

> Race has become a trope of ultimate, irreducible difference between cultures, linguistic groups, or adherents of specific belief systems which—more often than not—also have fundamentally opposed economic interests. Race is the ultimate trope of difference because it is so very arbitrary in its application. The biological criteria used to determine "difference" in sex simply do not hold when applied to "race." ("Writing 'Race' and the Difference It Makes" 1985, 5)

For Gates, the task of the Afro-American literary critic is, in part, to attend to the ways in which language (re)inscribes naturalizing or essentializing notions of "race," that is, to locate and to demystify the complicated and often dangerous ways in which "race" as a trope is scripted into our discursive formulations.

This deconstruction of "race" as an essential, natural, empirical category is precisely what Joyce A. Joyce objects to in the by now infamous *New Literary History* debate on Afro-American literary theory and criticism. She expresses general reservations about "the merger of Negro expression with Euro-American expression" ("The Black Canon" 1987a, 339), but specifically she objects to something ambiguously identified as "the poststructuralist sensibility." "The poststructuralist sensibility," she insists, "does not adequately apply to Black American literary works" (342). Critiquing the poststructuralist criticism of Gates and Baker, Joyce states her position: "I do not understand how a Black critic aware of the implantations of racist structures in the consciousness of Blacks and whites could accept poststructuralist ideas and practices" (" 'Who the Cap Fit' " 1987b, 379). Joyce holds the opinion that for Gates, Baker, or any other Afro-American critic to deconstruct "race" as a dominant conceptual category amounts to turning their backs on Afro-American culture, denying not merely their literary tradition but their very identity as black: "It is insidious for the Black literary critic to adopt any kind of strategy that diminishes or . . . negates his blackness" (1987a, 341). The charge, then, is clear: to deconstruct "race" is to abdicate, negate, or destroy black identity.

There are several ways to respond to this accusation, and the remainder of this chapter will address some of these possible responses. I will begin with a discussion of Anthony Appiah's philosophic approach to the question of "race" in order to demonstrate the extent to which Joyce Joyce's objections to poststructuralism are (not surprisingly) really objections to literary criticism's recent in-roads into philosophy. Next, I will address Henry Louis Gates, Jr.'s current work on translation and signification as two possible ways for rethinking the relation between European theory and Afro-American literature. And finally I will examine Houston Baker's "blues criticism" to uncover the materialist inscriptions of "race" in contemporary theory and its various modes of reinscription in political discourse. The chapter will conclude with my own suggestions for further study in the general field of Afro-American literary criticism.

Appiah's Apples

Appiah, Baker, and Gates do share at least one major concern with Joyce—a concern over exactly how the relation between Continental (white) theory and Afro-American literature is to be articulated. Of the three, Appiah is the most pessimistic about the possibilities for the *successful* union of Afro-American literary criticism and European philosophy—less because of cultural incompatibilities between the two than disciplinary ones. In Appiah's opinion, literary critics in general should avoid applying philosophical concepts or explanatory systems of any kind unless they are thoroughly versed in the conventions of philosophy. Appiah does not object to the use of Continental theory in reading African or Afro-American texts *per se*, but he does remain suspicious about *how* such theory is used by literary critics, and to what purpose.

Appiah's "Strictures on Structures: The Prospects for a Structuralist Poetics of African Fiction" (1984) provides us with the clearest articulation of the author's skeptical attitude toward structuralist and poststructuralist literary criticism. The article is a detailed critique of *Structural Models and African Poetics* by Sunday O. Anozie, an African structuralist whom Gates has dubbed "a veritable sub-Saharan Roland Barthes" ("Criticism in the Jungle" in Gates 1984, 16). Appiah is completely up-front about his expectations in approaching such a text (and any recent work of literary criticism):

> I do not come to a work of contemporary literary theory without presentiments. I anticipate a style of writing, and thought, which mistakes the obscure for the profound; which confuses a reading of philosophy with a philosophical reading; which dispenses, in fact, with the urge for clarity and reason that lies at the root of the philosophical tradition of the country from which so much darkness and unreason now emanates. Occasionally, I am pleasurably surprised, but rarely. In short, I expect little pleasure from such texts. (1984, 128)

What bothers Appiah is the *uncritical* application of philosophical theory to literary texts: "if literary theory is to gain anything from linguistics (or, for that matter, from philosophy), it cannot be indifferent to the question of the adequacy of the theories of which it makes use" (130–31). Appiah is careful to point out that the error and confusion which mar *Structural Models and African Poetics* derive not from Anozie but from the structuralist authors he cites; Anozie's chief failure is one of not being critical enough, of not being sufficiently rigorous and analytical, even, one might say, of not being enough of a philosopher.

If Appiah faults critics like Anozie for failing to be (adequate) philosophers, Joyce Joyce makes the correlative move and chastises Appiah for being too much of a philosopher and not enough of a literary (new) critic. Joyce cites a passage from Appiah's "The Uncompleted Argument: Du Bois and the Illusion of Race" as a representative example of the "quasi-scientific, alienating analyses" (1987b, 376) produced by contemporary critical discourse. Appiah, of course, is merely writing within the conventions of his own discourse, analytic philosophy, though Joyce implies that if Appiah is going to transgress into the field of Du Bois and Afro-American literature, then he needs to adopt a more "appropriate" language. For Joyce, philosophy and literature are two distinct disciplines; for Appiah, the matter is more complicated.

There is little question that the fields of contemporary philosophy (especially Continental philosophy) and literary criticism have been deeply involved of late—more than a passing flirtation—and sometimes passionately at odds. Few would disagree, I think, that "theory" has had a profound impact on contemporary literary studies (though there is by no means any consensus on whether this has been for the better or for the worse). And it is also generally acknowledged that literary theorists have made a significant contribution to the field of philosophical inquiry; "literary theory," after all, is as much "theory" as it is "literary." But this reciprocal influence has been partially if not wholly occluded by the tendency of philosophy to situate itself as, in Luce Irigaray's words, "the discourse on discourses" (1977a, 149)—in other words, as *the* master discourse. Historically, philosophy and literature have never been that far apart (one thinks of Lao Tsu's *Tao Te Ching*, Plato's *Republic*, *The Bhagavad Gita*, Mary Wollstonecraft's *The Vindication of the Rights of Woman*, Nietzsche's *Thus Spoke Zarathustra*, Emerson's *Nature*, Sartre's *Nausea*, Irigaray's "When Our Lips Speak Together"); their projects have often been, if not indistinguishable, then certainly complicit. Perhaps the recent territorial anxiety to demarcate the boundaries of philosophy and literary criticism (an anxiety that motivates both the Appiah and the Joyce pieces) is based on an underlying suspicion that philosophy and literature are caught in an Imaginary relation, that they are, in fact, so proximate as to be nearly the same.

This fear may account for Appiah's curious advice at the end of "Strictures on Structures" that "practical critics" should refrain from tinkering with "theory"; it is better for the literary critic to remain innocent of philosophy, he believes, than to eat of the poststructuralist apple and attain only an imperfect knowledge. Referring to the mix of philosophical confusion and skilled practical criticism which characterizes Anozie's *Structural Models and African Poetics*, Appiah concludes: "Those who read it will be confirmed in their 'reactionary' view that literary study is a matter not of the development of theory but of a sensitive understanding of literary texts. . . . I do not think this will be too bad a thing" (148). Appiah could be sending several messages to literary critics with such a cautionary if not protectionist position. "If you can't do philosophy adequately, please don't do it at all." Or, "become a philosopher if you wish to dabble in philosophy." Or maybe, "these days philosophers make the best literary critics"? Let me go one tentative step further: is Appiah's real fear not that philosophers make the best literary critics but rather, in a time when Derrida is more popular in departments of Literature than in departments of Philosophy, that literary critics make the best philosophers?[5]

It might be instructive to interrogate Appiah's own speaking position in this article on Anozie, one of Africa's best-known literary critics: does Appiah himself speak as a philosopher or as a literary critic? I believe he speaks as a philosopher who feels competent to judge literary criticism, or who, more accurately, feels no need to defend his right to do so. What remains unspoken is the very assumption that philosophy is the master discourse and that philosophers, operating on this premise, have no need to justify their crossing into other disciplines. What is striking about this debate between philosopher and literary critic (Appiah and Anozie) is the manifestations of transference it produces. Appiah situates himself in the role of "master analyst," analyzing the discourse of analysis itself, through a close (literary) reading of the texts of Sunday O. Anozie, the analysand in this encounter. Condescending in his praise of a naive practical criticism, Appiah's own critical discourse discloses the adversarial relation between philosopher and literary critic, or rather, between the philosopher who is *also* literary critic and the literary critic who is *also* philosopher. The chief weakness of Appiah's "Strictures on Structures" lies in his failure to interrogate his own countertransference onto the literary critic. Content to remain in the role of master philosopher, Appiah misses the chance both to provide an auto-critique of his own practice as literary critic and to confront his identification with Anozie, including the rivalry and aggressivity such identification engenders. Failure to acknowledge the transference and countertransference at play here leads Appiah to reinforce rather than to undermine the central philosophy/literature binarism—thereby reproducing the very structuralist thinking which he faults so persistently in Anozie's work. This doubling of Anozie's structuralism locks both parties into an Imaginary, or oppositional, encounter of mirror images; consequently, Appiah's reading of Anozie becomes, in the end, more of an appropriation than a self-aware critical intervention.

What I find most helpful and persuasive in Appiah's reading of Anozie is his attentiveness to the difficulties involved in reading African texts through European lenses:

> It is not that a structuralist poetics is inapplicable in Africa because structuralism is European; so far as it is successful in general, it seems to me as applicable to African literary material as to any other. But we should not expect the transfer of a method to a new set of texts to lead to exactly the same results . . . indeed, this would surely *show* that there was something wrong with the method. (145)

Appiah is wary of a certain "post-colonial legacy" he sees operative in Anozie's work, a legacy "which requires us to show that African literature is worthy of study precisely (but only) because it is fundamentally the same as European literature" (145). He calls this legacy "the Naipaul fallacy":

> Again and again, Anozie asks the reader to understand Africa by embedding it in European culture—a habit we might perhaps dub "the Naipaul fallacy." But what, save a post-colonial inferiority complex, would lead anyone into the assumption that this embedding is either necessary or desirable? (146)

Appiah's position is rightly cited by Henry Louis Gates, Jr. as a particularly useful way to think about Third World criticism,[6] but before shifting the discussion to Gates's understanding of poststructuralist Afro-American theory, let me simply emphasize that, in Appiah's view, the question of how "to mediate between Europe and Africa" must be theorized in relation to other associated questions. Specifically, to query the tie between European theory and African literature is symptomatic of another problem—the problem of the relation between philosophy and literary criticism—and to address the second question is in some way to speak more profoundly to the first.

Opening the Flood-Gates

Gates's notion of "translation" poses one important alternative or corrective to the "Naipaul fallacy." It is Gates who has perhaps done the most to open the flood-gates for poststructuralist Afro-American literary theory, primarily through his editorship of two important volumes: *Black Literature & Literary Theory* and *"Race," Writing, and Difference.* In his own contributions to these books, as well as in his remarks in *New Literary History* on the resistance to theory among Afro-American critics, Gates develops his theory of "translation" to answer the following question: "how 'applicable' is contemporary literary theory to the reading of the African, Caribbean and Afro-American literary traditions?" ("Criticism in the Jungle" 1984, 3). Gates ultimately concludes that any theory, any critical tool, which helps elucidate the Afro-American text is "applicable" and "appropriate," but not without adding the caveat that the critic who turns *only* to white Western literary and critical traditions, who fails to account for "indigenous black principles of criticism" ("What's Love Got To Do With It?" 1987b, 352), is simply "destined to recapitulate unwittingly the racist stereotype of Minstrel Man, a Tzvetan Todorov in black face" ("Talkin' That Talk" 1986b, 208).

Using Continental theory to write about Afro-American texts is not without its dangers: critics risk enslavement to yet another form of "intellectual indenture," and they risk entrapment in what Gates calls "a 'mockingbird' relation to theory, one destined to be derivative, often to the point of parody" (1987b, 349–50). But such views of Afro-American poststructuralist theory are predicated on a one-way relation, an understanding of criticism which views the literary text as somehow subordinate to the theoretical text and incapable of transforming that text in turn.

> Theory, like words in a poem, does not "translate" in a one-to-one relationship of reference. Indeed, I have found that, in the "application" of a mode of reading to black texts, the critic, by definition, transforms the theory and, I might add, transforms received readings of the text into something different, a construct neither exactly 'like' its antecedents nor entirely new. (1984, 4)

Translation, then, always involves transformation: "I have tried to work through contemporary theories of literature *not* to "apply" them to black texts, but rather to *transform* by *translating* them into a new rhetorical realm" (1987b, 351). If repetition is also involved in this process of translation, then surely, Gates insists, it is "repetition with a difference, a signifying black difference" (1984, 3).

Gates's very notion of translation repeats Derrida's understanding of this process—with a difference.[7] Both agree that translation is more than just a secondary operation.[7] Once a text has been translated, the "original" is no longer the same; it, too, has been changed by the operation of translation. As Derrida explains in *The Ear of the Other:*

Translation has nothing to do with reception or communication or information. . . . The translator must assure the survival, *which is to say the growth*, of the original, which, insofar as it is living on, never ceases to be transformed and to grow. It modifies the original even as it also modifies the translating language. This process—transforming the original as well as the translation—is the translation contract between the original and the translating text. (122)

Gates concurs: the critic of Afro-American literature who uses, say, Derridean deconstruction to read an Afro-American text "changes both the received theory and received ideas about the text" (1984, 9). What is different about Gates' conception of "translation" is that it must hold out the possibility of retranslation. "I have tried to write texts that don't return and don't allow for retranslation," Derrida writes; "a text, I believe, does not come back" (1982b, 157, 156). But given the Afro-American writer's dual audience, a translation is always, simultaneously, a retranslation—or perhaps more accurately, a *bi-translation:*

In the case of the writer of African descent, her or his texts occupy spaces in at least two traditions: a European or American literary tradition, and one of the several but related distinct, black traditions. The "heritage" of each black text written in a Western language is, then, a double heritage, two-toned, as it were. Its visual tones are white and black, and its aural tones are standard and vernacular. (1984, 4)

A critic involved in the interpretation of Afro-American texts is engaged in a complicated process of "bitranslation"—of translating in at least two directions at once (as the hyphenated "Afro-American" might suggest) and negotiating between at least two "ordinary" texts in need of mutual translation. The line between "original" and "translation" is never clear; indeed, to displace this privileged binarism in Western discourse may have already become the Afro-Americanist's special burden.

So how, exactly, is poststructuralist theory transformed by Afro-American literature? Here we need to turn from translation to signification, for it is the "signifying difference" of the Afro-American text which transforms our very (ethnocentric) theoretical understanding of what it means to signify. In "The Blackness of Blackness: A Critique of the Sign and the Signifying Monkey" (in Gates 1984),[8] Gates informs his white Western readers that the concept of signification which semioticians ordinarily associate with Ferdinand de Saussure has been a central part of the black vernacular tradition for more than two centuries. Signification, Gates demonstrates, is precisely the name for a traditional theory and practice of reading in Afro-American culture; "signification is the nigger's occupation," reads one popular saying in Afro-American folklore.[9] The Signifying Monkey is "black mythology's archetypal signifier" (286), a trickster figure who repeats and reverses at the same time—the king of chiasmus, one might say. But chiasmus, along with metaphor, metonymy, metalepsis, catachresis, hyperbole, and a chain of other figures, is a Western master-trope. Afro-American tradition provides us with a rather different series of signifying practices: " 'marking', 'loud-talking', 'specifying', 'testifying', 'calling out' (of one's name), 'sounding', 'rapping' and 'playing the dozens' " (286). Signifying as an Afro-American rhetorical practice, is, above all, "the slave's trope, the trope of tropes" (286) which allows the speaker to argue indirectly (through innuendo, humor, or riddles) and, sometimes, to undermine and to unbalance a master discourse. What is important about Gates's work on the "Signifying Monkey" is that it *historicizes* the very sign of signification itself; indeed, one of the most important contributions Afro-American criticism in general has made to semiotics is this rigorous impulse to historicize and to contextualize. Thus, in theorizing the relation between Afro-American criticism and contemporary literary theory, we need always to bear in mind that the "gates" swing both ways here.

Gates is himself something of a trickster figure as he "signifies upon" a largely white, Western critical discourse. I can think of no better example of Gates's deftness at signifying than his carefully chosen title for the introductory article to *Black Literature and Literary Theory*: "Criticism in the Jungle." Readers of Geoffrey Hartman will recognize Gates's play on Hartman's deconstructive text *Criticism in the Wilderness* (1980), and feminist readers will further identify Gates's troping on Elaine Showalter's revision of Hartman entitled "Feminist Criticism in the Wilderness" (1982). Both Gates and Showalter choose the same pre-text, as it were, upon which to mark their critical differences from the largely white, male literary tradition which Hartman's book represents. This highly influential and important book by a well-known Yale critic mentions only one woman writer in passing (Emily Dickinson) and no Afro-American writers at all. Because Hartman's wilderness turns out to be populated by white, male, mostly Western critics, Gates and Showalter share the important critical project of displacing a phallocentric, ethnocentric literary tradition. To the extent that Afro-American and feminist criticism both occupy a space outside the Outside, a wilderness beyond The Wilderness, they seem to be strategically allied and theoretically compatible critical schools. While this is partly true, if we compare a bit more closely Showalter's "Feminist Criticism in the Wilderness" and Gates's "Criticism in the Jungle," the asymmetry of the titles alone underscores some important theoretical disjunctures between them. For example, Showalter wishes to retain the controlling image of the wilderness while Gates replaces it altogether with the new spatial metaphor of the jungle. And while Showalter appends to "wilderness" the adjective "feminist," Gates deliberately omits the qualifier "Black" or "Afro-American." Some critics, like Joyce Joyce, undoubtedly see this erasure of "race" as symptomatic (symptomatic, that is, of a failure on Gates's part to acknowledge the importance of "race" in literary criticism), but clearly for Gates it is merely a way to defuse the essentializing connotations of "race" and, further, to avoid confusing "black critic" with the less ethnocentric "critic of black literature" (1986b, 207).

We can locate still other critical differences between Showalter and Gates. Most strikingly, Showalter advocates examining the literary text from virtually any theoretical perspective *but* the semiotic, whereas Gates privileges semiotic interpretation, if semiotics is here taken to mean the study of signifying practices.[10] Gates's interest in the sign "black" and its discursive production in literary texts sets him apart not just from the "early" Showalter but from the mainstream of contemporary Afro-American criticism. Gates believes that "a study of the so-called arbitrariness of the sign, of the ways in which *concepts* divide reality arbitrarily, and of the relation between a sign, such as blackness, and its referent, such as absence, can help us to engage in more sophisticated readings of black texts" (1984, 7). But this semiotic approach is met with charges that poststructuralist Afro-American theory de-socializes and de-politicizes the text. The "New Black Formalism," Norman Harris writes, "disfigures the literature it discusses while trivializing the dreams and aspirations of Afro-Americans in the world" (" 'Who's Zoomin' Who' " 1987, 39). According to Harris, "there must be some essence which precedes and/or transcends the fact of objective conditions" (41). To de-essentialize "race" by treating it as a sign is seen to cut loose Afro-American literature from its cultural moorings; "the terms derived from Afro-American culture become meaningless and whorelike" (40). R. Baxter Miller, in a reading of the politics of "play" in Afro-American criticism, indicts the poststructuralists for self-indulgence, elitism, pedantry, scholarly jargon, faddishness, and fraternalism. Gates, remarkably, is identified by Miller as "a leading neo-conservative among Afro-American intellectuals today"

("Baptized Infidel" 1987, 412). For this influential Afro-American critic, "what is most fascinating about some contemporary Afro-American play is that, while the critical narrative is explicitly radical or avant-garde, it is implicitly quite reactionary" (395).

I dwell at length on these specific criticisms of the work of both Henry Louis Gates, Jr. and Houston A. Baker, Jr. since they seem to me representative of the backlash against theory which Gates has himself already addressed in his published response to Joyce Joyce. I wish to add a word or two more to Gates's own self-defense. All of these criticisms of poststructuralist Afro-American theory are concerned with preserving the "authentic" nature of the Afro-American text. All are wary that a preoccupation with language will de-nature black literature and culture, detach the text from its cultural roots. All attempt, in other words, to hold fast to the bedrock of essentialism. One way to counter these charges is to show how racial essentialism is exactly that which historically underwrites cultural racism and which tenaciously upholds its academic institutionalization (for example, in ethnocentric theories of canonization). Another point that must surely be made is that language and culture are hardly opposed; the claim that a concentration on language ignores material culture misinterprets the materiality of language and the semiology of culture. To read Gates's re-historicization of the sign "black" as an act of de-historicization suppresses the crucial fact that race is itself a historical construction. I will have more to say about this in the next section on Houston Baker's blues criticism. Although their positions frequently differ, Baker has been subject to many of the same criticisms Gates inevitably seems to provoke. As I hope to show, the charges of amaterialism are particularly misguided when leveled against Baker, a critic whose attentiveness to the social and political meanings of race, and to the concrete social relations in which they are embedded, mark his work as profoundly materialist.

Baker's Blues

In a revised version of one of his most influential pieces, "Generational Shifts and the Recent Criticism of Afro-American Literature,"[11] Houston Baker identifies three general (and generational) movements of the past forty years in Afro-American literary criticism: the "Integrationists" of the 1950s and early 1960s (Richard Wright, Sterling Brown, Arthur P. Davis, Ulysses Lee) who sought entry into the mainstream of American culture; the "Black Aestheticians" of the 1960s and 1970s (Addison Gayle, Jr., Stephen Henderson, the "early" Houston

Baker) who advocated a literary cultural nationalism; and, finally, the "Reconstructionists" of the late 1970s and early 1980s (Robert B. Stepto, Henry Louis Gates, Jr.) who practiced semiotic, structuralist readings of Afro-American texts. It is clear that Baker's own affinities lie, even now, with the Black Aestheticians, in large part because "a Black Aesthetic generation was the first paradigmatic community to demonstrate the efficacy of the vernacular" (112). Yet Baker pioneers a fourth generational movement which, in its use of European theory, its attention to black culture and the vernacular, and its concentration on the formal workings of the text, combines and utilizes all three of the earlier approaches to Afro-American literature. This fourth approach might be labeled "blues criticism"; as blues critic, Houston Baker riffs on the earlier notes in Afro-American literary criticism and sounds a new note for contemporary poststructuralist theory.[12]

The blues, Baker tells us, seem "always to have been in motion in America—always becoming, shaping, transforming, displacing the peculiar experiences of Africans in the New World" (5). As we have seen in Chapter One, Baker goes even further and describes the blues as the "always already" of Afro-American culture (4); it is the task of the blues critic to *translate* this quasi-mystical "always already" of Afro-American culture for a blues audience, to become, in effect, a blues singer in order to "situate himself productively at the crossroads" and thereby to produce what Baker calls "translation at the crossing" (202). Perhaps the most recurrent image in the blues is that of the railroad crossing, for the blues represent virtually a railroad genre, sung originally at Southern railway junctures before they were "discovered" by W. C. Handy in 1903. What attracts Baker to the blues as a useful way to talk about Afro-American poststructuralist theory is its obvious connection to the black vernacular, on the one hand, and its less perceptible but equally provocative ties to signification on the other. The blues operate in Afro-American culture as a figure for *différance,* if we think of *différance* most simply as "the 'active,' moving discord of different forces" (Derrida 1972b, 18). Speaking of the blues, Baker writes: "even as they speak of paralyzing absence and ineradicable desire, their instrumental rhythms suggest change, movement, action, continuance, unlimited and unending possibility. Like signification itself, blues are always nomadically wandering. Like the freight-hopping hobo, they are ever on the move, ceaselessly summing novel experience" (8).

The two figures in Baker's work that come to stand most centrally for *différance* are the railway roundhouse and the crossing sign. The roundhouse, located at the center of the switchyard, switches trains from track to track. One thinks of Derrida's notion of "switch points" elaborated in *The Post Card*. Switch points are those linguistic levers which insure that words and letters never reach their final destinations; instead, they are intercepted, detoured, relayed. "I love the delicate levers which pass between the legs of a word, between a word and itself to the point of making entire civilizations seesaw," Derrida writes (1980, 78). The railroad crossing sign also functions as a signal for a certain Derridean notion of ceaseless movement and play; for Baker, "the crossing sign is the antithesis of a place marker. It signifies, always, change, motion, transience, process" (202). The railroad blues thus become a possible *site* of *différance* in Afro-American culture:

> The railway juncture is marked by transience. Its inhabitants are always travelers—a multifarious assembly in transit. The 'x' of cross-ing roadbeds signals the multi-directionality of the juncture and is simply a single instance in a boundless network that redoubles and circles, makes sidings and ladders, forms Y's and branches over the vastness of hundreds of thousands of American miles. Polymorphous and multidirectional, scene of arrivals and departures, place betwixt and between (ever *entre les deux*), the juncture is the way-station of the blues. (7)

It is important to note here that railway junctions take on specific historical signification for Afro-Americans; they symbolize the physi-cal, material displacement of millions of Southern sharecroppers, in the late 19th and early 20th centuries, migrating by trains to the North in search of jobs, safety, and a less racist environment.

Siting the blues within a Derridean framework can be a useful exer-cise in that it provides us with a specifically Afro-American translation of *différance*, but reading Derrida through the prism of American blues can also be instructive. Translation, after all, works both ways; "call and response" can always be reversed, with striking results. It is tempt-ing to think of Derrida as one of Baker's "freight-hopping hobos," and indeed *The Post Card*, with its recurrent train imagery, encourages us to do so. What happens if we relocate Derrida, sidetrack him if you will, from a Parisian metro car to a Southern railway boxcar, from the European Orient Express to an Afro-American soul train? One of the things which we learn is that Derrida is a master at improvisation; he strikes a favorite tune and replays it, with significant variations, over and over again. "Still the same book," he confesses in *The Post Card*, "and I am incapable of writing anything else" (1980, 92). We also uncover a preoccupation with *sound* in the Derridean corpus—particu-larly the sound of words:

> The word guard [garde]: at this second I love it, I tell it that I love it,
> I also like to say it to myself, make it sing, let the *a* drag on for a long
> time, stretch it out at length, it is the voice, my vowel, the most
> *marked* letter, everything begins with it. (1980, 82)

The image of Derrida as blues musician, a Parisian John Coltrane, is
not merely a fanciful transposition (though it is partly that); it tells us
a great deal about the improvisational energy and instrumental play
generated by the deconstructor at work.

Baker, then, refining Gates's vision of the scholar as trickster, gives
us an image of the critic as hobo, "a liminal trickster always on the
move" (200). If Derrida thinks of himself as a royal courier or a long-
distance marathon runner, Baker pictures himself as a blues singer
riding the freight trains of vernacular tradition and continually switch-
ing tracks at the critical crossroads. Indeed, the most scenic and challenging place for an Afro-American critic to be these days, according
to Baker, is at the twin junctures of Afro-American literature and
European theory, as well as at the crossroads where the formal and
vernacular traditions in Afro-American culture meet. "The task of
present day scholars," Baker suggests, "is to situate themselves inven-
tively and daringly at the crossing sign in order to materialize vernacular faces" (202). Baker's literary criticism is pre-eminently materialist;
he is interested in "the 'production' and 'modes of production' that
foregrounds Afro-American labor" (3) and he is fundamentally concerned with questions of politics, history, and ideology, particularly
as they relate to the economics of slavery and to the sound of the
vernacular.

Baker's chief criticism of *"Race," Writing, and Difference,* and of
Gates's editorial choices in particular, reflects a deep concern for the
status of the vernacular in contemporary theory:

> "Subtle" modes of contemporary analysis, the editor implies, will
> somehow unify a group of commentators on issues as traditionally
> divisive as race and Otherness. At the same instant, he suggests that
> *only* individualizing vernacular models can make sense of such issues.
> There is confusion. ("Caliban's Triple Play" 1986, 184)

Gates, in fact, calls for an Afro-American literary criticism which will
attend to *both* the black vernacular and contemporary theory; his logic
is that of both/and rather than either/or. Such a logic need not signal
confused thinking or methodological wishy-washiness, or if it does
produce a form of chaos, then it is an immensely productive chaos

which has generated the two fine volumes, *Black Literature & Literary Theory* and *"Race," Writing, and Difference,* as Baker would surely agree. But Baker's charge is more serious than this; he worries that those "'subtle' modes of contemporary analysis" have already begun to *subsume* the vernacular, to the point where "the vernacular seems to become almost a tag" (1986, 184–85). What we see in the work of both Gates and Baker is a romanticization of the vernacular. As their detractors have been all too quick to point out, each of these critics speaks *about* the black vernacular but rarely can they be said to speak *in* it (in the same way that some feminist critics can be said to speak about but not in *écriture féminine*). A powerful *dream* of the vernacular motivates the work of these two Afro-Americanists, perhaps because, for the professionalized literary critic, the vernacular has already become irrevocably lost. What makes the vernacular (the language of "the folk") so powerful a theme in the work of both Gates and Baker is precisely the fact that it operates as a phantasm, a hallucination of lost origins. It is in the quest to recover, reinscribe, and revalorize the black vernacular that essentialism inheres in the work of two otherwise anti-essentialist theorists. The key to blackness is not visual but *auditory;* essentialism is displaced from sight to sound.

To prevent any possible muffling of an essential vernacular sound in Afro-American poststructuralist theory, Baker advocates holding onto a concept of race which will allow us to survey "the valleys and lowgrounds of Blackness" (*Afro-American Poetics,* 101). The vernacular has a sound, "a defiantly *racial* sound" (95), produced both by the cacophonous, invigorating noises of the slogans, songs, and chants of the Civil Rights/Black Power movements, and by the soul and folk music of the American South, including the blues. "These quotidian sounds of black every day life become a people's entrancing song" (107), Baker explains in his discussion of that great mystical novel, Jean Toomer's *Cane.* Baker believes that it is difficult to comprehend the sound of Toomer's *Cane* without understanding the importance of "trance" and its central place in the literature of the Harlem Renaissance.[13] But what, exactly, is meant by trance? Baker thinks of trance as a "mediumistic mode" (102) which allows Afro-American writers and critics to tune into "the almost inaudible levels of Afro-American discourse that mark a distinctive black poetic experience in America" (98). The critic as medium becomes an agent of transmission and translation, a spokesperson whose job is to safeguard race from those who wish, not to deconstruct it, but to silence its political voice. The word itself becomes a useful tool to Baker, as the following word game will, I think, make clear. If we remove the letter "n" from "trance," we have the word "trace"; and if we further drop the letter "t," we have "race." Linguistically, there is always a trace of race in trance. Baker has no wish to put "race" under erasure; his concept of "trance" is designed precisely in order to reinscribe race discursively in his own critical productions.

Baker's materialist poststructuralism permits him the possibility of retaining "race" as a *political* category, if nothing else. His critique of Anthony Appiah's work on Du Bois suggests that any critical position which successfully deconstructs "race" as an empirical fact but fails to account for its continuing political efficacy is ultimately inadequate:

> Depression quickly sets in when one realizes that what Appiah—in harmony with his privileged evolutionary biologists—discounts as mere "gross" features of hair, bone, and skin are not, in fact, discountable. In a world dramatically conditioned both by the visible and by a perduring discursive formation of "old" (and doubtless mistaken) racial enunciative statements, such gross features always make a painfully significant difference—perhaps, *the only* significant difference where life and limb are concerned in a perilous world. (1986, 185)

In some ways, the Appiah / Baker debate recapitulates an exchange between Peggy Kamuf and Nancy K. Miller on the question of the signature, a feminist debate played out on the pages of *Diacritics* in 1982.[14] Appiah, in effect, sides with Kamuf, arguing that to affix a racial signified to the signature is to assign intentionality to the text and thus to contain and to foreclose it. Baker's position more closely approximates Miller's, for he holds that the signature's racial signified *does* matter, historically, politically, and materially, and has always affected the conditions of production, reception, and survival of texts written by Afro-Americans. Appiah wishes to eradicate "race" as an empirical term in biologizing discourses, while Baker seeks to retain "race" as a political term in literary and critical discourses. These two gestures, I would submit, are only apparently contradictory. There is no reason why "race" should be performing, *essentially,* the same function across discourses; "race" is a variable and flexible term. But even if we do wish to attribute to "race" always and everywhere the same fixed meaning (a difficult project in and of itself), we can still work with "race" as a political concept *knowing* it is a biological fiction.

To say that "race" is a biological fiction is not to deny that it has real material effects in the world; nor is it to suggest that "race" should disappear from our critical vocabularies. Clearly it is no more adequate to hold that "race" is itself merely an empty effect than it is to insist that "race" is solely a matter of skin color. What is called for is a closer look at the production of racial subjects, at what forces organize, administer, and produce racial identities. What is called for is an approach which intervenes in the essentialist/constructionist polemic that has hitherto imprisoned "race" in a rigidified and falsifying logic. On the one hand, to maintain a strict constructionist view which holds that there is no such thing in racial identity can block our understanding of the social production of "race." On the other hand, to advocate an even more rigid essentialist view which holds that "race" is self-evidently hereditary or biologistic can also interfere with an analysis of the ideological and political formation of racial subjects. Neither a pure constructionist approach nor an unalloyed essentialist one is sufficiently equipped to come to grips with a question as theoretically complex and politically urgent as the place and function of "race" in the era of poststructuralism. In light of the current debates on the meaning of "race" (not only in literary criticism but in many other academic fields as well), perhaps what we need to explore most urgently is the *history of the sign* "race"—as Michael Omi and Howard Winant have attempted to do in their excellent study, *Racial Formation in the United States* (1986). Such historically specific studies remind us that racial categories are politically shaped, that "race consciousness" is a modern phenomenon, and that the very meaning of "race" has shifted over time and across cultures.[15] The current tensions and disputes surrounding "race" (the complexity of which this chapter has only begun to uncover) powerfully demonstrate that "race" is an important site of intense political contestation. These debates also confirm that there was little if any agreement to begin with on the question of what "race" signifies, and, further, that no theory of "race" can be extracted fully from the ideological and social contexts which produced it.

There is another powerful argument to be made in favor of holding onto the term "race," even though we may recognize its essentializing usages. It could be argued that one way to avoid what Gayatri Spivak has aptly labeled the problem of "chromatism," the problem of reducing race to a question of skin color (1986, 235), is to drop investigations of race in favor of analyses of ethnicity. Race, along with language, religion, nationality, geography, and other social factors, could function as simply one of several determinants of ethnic identity.[16] But to see "Blackness" as an ethnic marker (equivalent to Germanness or Jewishness) has historically worked to homogenize black identity, to de-particularize the black subject: "ethnicity theory isn't very interested in ethnicity *among* blacks. The ethnicity approach views blacks as one ethnic group among others. It does not consider national origin, religion, language, or cultural differences among blacks, as it does among whites, as sources of ethnicity" (Omi and Winant 1986, 23). Moreover, to substitute "ethnicity" for "race" would be to e-race, if you will, the rich and color-full history of "race" in Afro-American culture; the "race men" and "race women" of Afro-American history and politics would fade into the background, effaced by the more neutral, less politically evocative term "ethnicity." In American culture, "race" has been far more an acknowledged component of black identity than white; for good or bad, whites have always seen "race" as a minority attribute, and blacks have courageously and persistently agitated on behalf of "the race." It is easy enough for white poststructuralist critics to place under erasure something they *think* they never had to begin with. I think this is the fear that motivates Baker's recent attack on Anthony Appiah's support of the evolutionary biologists:

> The scenario they seem to endorse reads as follows: when science apologizes and says there is no such thing [as "race"], all talk of "race" must cease. Hence "race," as a recently emergent, unifying, and forceful sign of difference *in the service* of the "Other," is held up to scientific ridicule as, ironically, "unscientific." A proudly emergent sense of ethnic diversity in the service of new world arrangements is disparaged by whitemale science as the most foolish sort of anachronism. (1986, 186)

What Baker fears most is a science which lacks "present-day political sensitivity" and which denies "'real side' referentiality" (1986, 188). Baker is above all concerned with race's sociohistorical inscriptions and political effects. Far from engaging in ahistorical or apolitical hermeneutics, Baker's work calls for a radical historicization of "race" and a persistent interrogation of racial ideologies. Because of the attentiveness to the way in which culture shapes consciousness, and sociopolitical relations produce "race," such a project cannot be dismissed lightly. Exposing the political and ideological investments within the very term "race" may offer one of the most effective means for combating racism wherever we may find it, including the seemingly neutral field of literary studies.

Afro-American Subjectivity

I have tried to show in this chapter some of the common themes as well as divergent philosophies which energize the work of three prominent theorists of race: Anthony Appiah, Henry Louis Gates, Jr., and Houston A. Baker, Jr. The work of these three theorists has collectively shifted attention away from sociological and thematic modes of reading—essentialist critical practices embedded in the Southern Agrarian racism of the American New Critics (see Gates 1985, 4)—and towards modes of reading more concerned with signification, ideology, and culture. W. Lawrence Hogue's recent call for an Afro-American literary criticism more attentive to literary production—to "the role played by the dominant cultural apparatus and Afro-American critical practices in producing and repressing, and therefore determining the shape of, Afro-American texts" (1986, 43)—has already been met by Houston Baker's *Blues, Ideology, and Afro-American Literature: A Vernacular Theory*, Henry Louis Gates, Jr.'s *The Signifying Monkey* (1988) and Hazel V. Carby's *Reconstructing Womanhood: The Emergence of the Afro-American Woman Novelist* (1987), to name just a few recent titles.[17] Hazel Carby's work is especially important for its attentiveness to the complex political formations and social conditions in which black women's literature has historically been produced. Carby's semiotic/materialist approach, grounded in British Cultural Studies, challenges us to rethink the category of "black feminist criticism" outside the essentialist and ahistorical frame in which it is often cast and, at the same time, compels us to interrogate the essentialism of traditional feminist historiography which posits a universalizing and hegemonizing notion of global sisterhood. Pressed to identify the predominant mode of criticism, then, in poststructuralist Afro-American literary theory today, I would say it is materialism, with discourse theory running a close second.[18]

In general, Afro-American literary critics have expressed little interest in reader-response approaches to Afro-American texts; Joe Weixlmann has already pointed out the conspicuous absence of any reader-response articles in Gates's anthology *Black Literature and Literary Theory,* an anthology he believes is heavily weighted towards structuralism ("Black Literary Criticism at the Junctures" 1986, 55).[19] Psychoanalytic readings in the field of Afro-American literary criticism are also hard to find, perhaps because of a widespread suspicion that psychoanalysis (arguably unlike Marxism) is a middle-class, ethnocentric discourse. Stepping back and surveying Afro-American poststructuralist theory as a whole, another omission leaps immediately to our attention, one with far more disturbing implications: the relative absence of Afro-American *feminist* poststructuralism. With the exception of the recent work of Hazel Carby and Hortense Spillers, black feminist critics have been reluctant to renounce essentialist critical positions and humanist literary practices.[20] What accounts exactly for the apparent resistance on the part of many minority women critics to what Barbara Christian has labeled "the race for theory" (1988)? How are we to read the complicated and subtle sexual dynamics at play beneath the surface of the *New Literary History* debate? Do Joyce Joyce's and Barbara Christian's impassioned repudiations of "theory" necessarily warrant the counter-charge of "a new black conservatism" amongst black women critics (Baker 1987, 367)? If such a conservatism can be convincingly established (conservative in comparison to what? one might legitimately ask), then is it possible that there might be an order of political necessity to these more essentialist arguments advanced by black women? These are difficult questions, for reasons not the least of which is the highly charged emotional and political climate in which they are posed, but they are also intractably insistent ones.

I would like to suggest, by way of concluding this discussion of race and essentialism, that one area worth pursuing in Afro-American theory, an area that has received little attention so far, is the question of subjectivity. How is black subjectivity constituted? According to Lacanian psychoanalysis, we all begin as divided subjects, but is the relationship of Afro-American subjectivity to social text fundamentally the same or different from Anglo-American subjectivity? Nancy K. Miller has argued in another context that the female subject's relation to desire, authority, and even textuality is *structurally* different from the male subject's: women do not necessarily have the same historical relation to identity; they have not necessarily felt "burdened by too much Self, Ego, Cogito"; and they do not necessarily start from a humanist fantasy of wholeness ("Changing the Subject" 1986a, 106). Might we say the same about the Afro-American subject, or is a rather different notion of subjectivity at work? It does seem plausible that, like the female subject, the Afro-American subject (who may also be female) *begins* fragmented and dispersed, begins with a "double-consciousness," as Du Bois would say (1903, 215). If so, then for both the female subject and the Afro-American subject, "the condition of dispersal and fragmentation that Barthes valorizes (and fetishizes) is not to be achieved but to be overcome" (Miller 1986a, 109).[21] It may well be that, impervious to processes of identity formation other than that of the *sexed* subject, Lacan's theory of subject constitution can only be of limited usefulness to theorists of race or of class. In any case, I think we still need to take Andreas Huyssen's concern seriously: "doesn't poststructuralism," he asks, "where it simply denies the subject altogether, jettison the chance of challenging the ideology of the subject (as male, white, and middle-class) by developing alternative and different notions of subjectivity?" (1984, 44). Developing these "alternative and different notions" to question current ethnocentric theories of the subject may well be one of the most important and urgent tasks facing the critic of Afro-American literature today.

Questions of identity and subjectivity emerge as particularly important questions to those groups historically denied access to the ego or the cogito. Though I have chosen to examine the question of "identity politics" in the next chapter on gay and lesbian theory, the politics of identity has operated as a vital political stratagem in virtually all of the social movements of the 20th Century, including the Civil Rights Movement in the U.S. and the many struggles for national liberation throughout the world. Much of what I will have to say about "identity politics" applies to these other social collectivities, but many of my remarks will also be quite specific to gay and lesbian communities. More work still needs to be done on the way in which identity politics both unites disparate social groups on the basis of shared political strategies and goals, but also frustrates the possibilities for successful "coalition politics" by insisting on the mutually exclusive nature of these identities.

6

Lesbian and Gay Theory:
The Question of Identity Politics

Few other issues have been as divisive and as simultaneously energizing in gay and lesbian theory as the question of whether "gay identity" is empirical fact or political fiction. Amongst political organizers in the gay movement, the notion of a gay essence is relied upon to mobilize and to legitimate gay activism; "gay pride," "gay culture," "gay sensibility" are all summoned as cornerstones of the gay community, indices of the emergence of a long-repressed collective identity. Recent gay theory, on the other hand, has increasingly rejected any such adherence to a natural, essential, or universal gay identity and emphasized instead "the making of the modern homosexual"[1]—that is, the way in which the homosexual subject is produced not naturally but discursively, across a multiplicity of discourses. The discourse theory of Michel Foucault has had perhaps the most profound and perceptible impact on the emerging field(s) of gay and lesbian theory; Foucault's efforts to de-essentialize sexuality and to historicize homosexuality as a modern "invention" have set the stage for the current disputes amongst gay theorists and activists over the meaning and applicability of such categories as "gay," "lesbian," and "homosexual" in a poststructuralist climate which renders all such assertions of identity problematic.

Central to the controversy over the invention theory of homosexuality is the related issue of "identity politics," a phrase with notably wide currency in gay and lesbian communities. In common usage, the term identity politics refers to the tendency to base one's politics on a sense of personal identity—as gay, as Jewish, as Black, as female. . . . Identity politics has been taken up by gay activists as something of a rallying cry to stimulate personal awareness and political action. It has been endorsed by both gay men and lesbians as a working theoretical base upon which to build a cohesive and visible political community. While the present study of identity politics does not wish to minimize or to deny its obvious utility as an organizational and political tool, it does wish to interrogate the analytical assumptions embedded in this concept and to investigate the role essentialism has played to keep it in circulation. It is my intent to trace briefly the historical and cultural construction of identity politics and, in particular, to decode the sometimes abstract and fuzzy notion of identity upon which this theory frequently depends. The project of historicizing "identity" seems especially appropriate in an investigation of the sign "homosexual" since the category of the "homo" is so often defined precisely as the identical or the same. Identity, allied with sameness, unity, and oneness, is commonly dismissed in poststructuralist feminist theory as simply another phallocratic concept,[2] but what I will suggest here is that identity is rarely identical to itself but instead has multiple and sometimes contradictory meanings. Another complementary tendency in current theory is to conflate "identity" with "essence" as if they were mirror images of each other—essentially the same, essentially identical. But identity, of course, has a philosophical and intellectual history of its own which, though it frequently dovetails with the history of the Western understanding of essence, nonetheless just as frequently trajects in quite different directions.

It should be clarified at the outset that although identity politics has been embraced by both lesbian and gay theorists, this is not to say that gay and lesbian subjects, as I have linked them together here, inevitably share the same concerns or necessarily represent a unified political coalition. Indeed, a certain adversarial relation between them (first and foremost, perhaps, on the level of theory) cannot be easily ignored—a tension I will return to at the end of this chapter. For now let me risk a tentative generalization which will partially explain the chapter's organizational frame. In general, current lesbian theory is less willing to question or to part with the idea of a "lesbian essence" and an identity politics based on this shared essence. Gay male theorists, on the other hand, following the lead of Foucault, have been quick to endorse the social constructionist hypothesis and to develop more detailed analyses of the historical construction of sexualities. That lesbian scholarship tends, on the whole, to be more essentialist than gay male scholarship is *not* to imply that lesbian theory is unsophisticated or reactionary; it is simply to suggest that if the adherence to essentialism is a measure of the degree to which a particular political group has been culturally oppressed (as this study has implied throughout), then the stronger lesbian endorsement of identity and identity politics may well indicate that lesbians inhabit a more precarious and less secure subject position than gay men. Lesbians, in other words, simply may have more to lose by failing to subscribe to an essentialist philosophy. This might explain, in part, the scarcity of Foucauldian analyses on lesbian sexuality compared to the plethora of such studies on the gay male subject—studies by Jeffrey Weeks (1977, 1985, 1986), David Halperin (1986), Gary Kinsman (1987), John D'Emilio (1983), and Simon Watney (1987), to name just a few.[3] I will be addressing the strengths and weaknesses of these social constructionist analyses shortly, but let me begin by examining the history and role of identity in current lesbian theorizations of identity politics.

The Politics of "Identity Politics"

One of the earliest endorsements amongst lesbian-feminists of the idea of identity politics can be found in the manifesto of the Combahee River Collective, a black lesbian activist group mobilized around the issues of sexual, racial, economic, and heterosexual oppressions:

> This focusing upon our own oppression is embodied in the concept of identity politics. We believe that the most profound and potentially the most radical politics come directly out of our own identity, as opposed to working to end somebody else's oppression ("A Black Feminist Statement" 1982, 16)[4]

Six years later, Chicana theorist Cherríe Moraga revised and expanded the concept to incorporate the growing recognition within feminist communities that an oppressed subject can also, simultaneously, be an oppressing subject: "the Radical Feminist must extend her own 'identity' politics to include her 'identity' as oppressor as well" (1983, 128). Identity politics finds its very roots in a radical feminism which draws its strength and staying power from a receptivity to cultural differences. It is by no means accidental that some of the most impassioned ratifications of the idea of an identity politics come from women of color: "As Black women we have an identity and therefore a politics that requires faith in the humanness of Blackness and femaleness. We are flying in the face of white male conceptions of what humanness is and proving that it is not them, but us."[5] The speaker is Barbara Smith, and her statement clarifies the precise nature of the relation between identity and politics: "we have an identity and *therefore* a politics." The link between identity and politics is causally and teleologically defined; for practitioners of identity politics, identity *necessarily* determines a particular kind of politics.

Given the causal relation established between "identity" and "politics," a certain pressure is applied to the lesbian subject to either "claim" or to "discover" her true identity before she can elaborate a "personal politics." In both gay and lesbian literature, a familiar tension emerges between a view of identity as that which is always there (but has been buried under layers of cultural repression) and that which has never been socially permitted (but remains to be formed, created, or achieved). Some writers shift from one position to the other with relative ease, incognizant of any contradictions generated by the juxtaposition of two radically different assumptions:

> Only women can give to each other a new sense of self. That identity we have to develop with reference to ourselves, and not in relation to men. . . . Together we must find, reinforce, and validate our authentic selves. (Radicalesbians 1973, 245)

This tension between the notions of "developing" an identity and "finding" an identity points to a more general confusion over the very definition of "identity" and over the precise signification of "lesbian." Some of the many creative and frequently incompatible definitions of "lesbian" have already been discussed in Chapter Three; what interests me here are the questions left unanswered by the seemingly natural appeal to a lesbian identity as a ready sanction and a secure platform for a lesbian politics.

What is missing in many of the treatises on lesbian identity is a recognition of the precarious status of identity and a full awareness of the complicated processes of identity formation, both psychical and social. What is missing is a concentrated focus upon the very terms which constitute an "identity politics," that is, an investigation of the shifting grounds marked not only by the slippery notion of identity but by the elusive status of politics as well. A series of unanswered questions pose themselves as central to any current discussion of identity politics. Is politics based on identity, or is identity based on politics? Is identity a natural, political, historical, psychical, or linguistic construct? What implications does the deconstruction of "identity" have for those who espouse an identity politics? Can feminist, gay, or lesbian subjects afford to dispense with the notion of unified, stable identities or must we begin to base our politics on something other than identity? What, in other words, is the politics of "identity politics"?

To Jenny Bourne, the politics of "identity politics" is always reactionary—reactionary because it fosters an apolitical, amaterialist, and subjectivist point of view. Bourne provides us with the most unrelenting, impassioned, and indeed courageous indictment of identity politics in a political climate which has elevated the achievement of identity to the very status of liberation:

> Identity Politics is all the rage. Exploitation is out (it is extrinsically determinist). Oppression is in (it is intrinsically personal). What is to be done has been replaced by who am I. Political culture has ceded to cultural politics. The material world has passed into the metaphysical. (1987, 1)

The root of the problem with identity politics, according to Bourne, can be attributed to a blind faith amongst those on the left in the feminist dictum, "the personal is political." Bourne writes: "the organic relationship we tried to forge between the personal and the political has been so degraded that now the only area of politics deemed to be legitimate *is* the personal" (2).[6] I find Bourne's rigorous critique of identity politics compelling and persuasive, if not, perhaps, occasionally overstated: "the tendency in feminist practice to personalise and internalise political issues . . . has created a stunted, inward-looking and self-righteous 'politics' which sets its face against the politics out there in the real world" (18–19).[7]

We should not, however, lose sight of the historical importance of a slogan which galvanized and energized an entire political movement. Initially, the claim "the personal is political" operated as a gravitational point for attracting attention to minority group concerns previously dismissed as personal grievances or isolated complaints. Demonstrating that the discontent of such groups originate not in personal or communal failure but in concrete social oppression necessitated expanding the sense of the political to encompass a much broader range of lived experience. But the problem with attributing political significance to every personal action is that the political is soon voided of any meaning or specificity at all, and the personal is paradoxically de-personalized. While I do believe that living as a gay or lesbian person in a post-industrial heterosexist society has certain political effects (whether I wish my sexuality to be so politically invested or not), I also believe that simply *being* gay or lesbian is not sufficient to constitute political activism. A severe reduction of the political to the personal leads to a telescoping of goals, a limiting of revolutionary activity to the project of self-discovery and personal transformation. "The personal is political" re-privatizes social experience, to the degree that one can be engaged in political praxis without ever leaving the confines of the bedroom. Sexual desire itself becomes invested with macropolitical significance. The personal, I am arguing, is *not* political, in any literal or equivalent fashion. It might be more useful to see the relation between these two terms as a complex co-implication rather than a simple equation. In any case, challenging the reduction of the political to the personal is a necessary first step towards re-assessing and *re-politicizing* "identity politics."

Theorizing Identity

The question of identity formation cannot be easily dismissed, much as we might wish to suspend or to defer such questions in the interest of shoring up our often beleaguered and embattled political positions. In fact, at no other time in the history of feminist theory has identity been at once so vilified and so sanctified; there is no middle ground, it seems, on the question of the contemporary status of identity and its importance to our theory and to our politics. What I propose to do here is to re-theorize, in effect, the "identity" of identity politics by re-historicizing the politics of various theories of identity. In other words, it may be possible to revise the popular understanding of the relation between identity and politics by rethinking the philosophical and linguistic gap between them. If we reject the tendency to base a politics on any unitary, stable, and coherent notion of identity, it may also be unwise to treat identity as fundamentally or solely a political construct. My own position will endorse the Lacanian understanding of identity as alienated and fictitious, and it will argue for the usefulness of seeing all representations of identity as simultaneously possible and impossible.

Questions of sameness and difference lie at the very heart of traditional metaphysical investigations into the problem of identity. To locate the identity of an object, for example, entails in analytic philosophy determining both whether that object is itself and not a different entity and whether that object remains the same over time.[8] In Aristotelian logic, essence and identity are closely related but by no means synonymous: a person or object possesses an essence which determines its identity, but identity, rather than operating as a substitute for essence, functions as its effect. Given Derrida's recent efforts to deconstruct "essence," this distinction becomes all the more crucial since it allows us to pose a more interesting question— namely, is it possible to base identity on something other than essence? While analytic philosophers continue to search for various criteria of identity,[9] Derrida's concurrent displacement of identity (as a stable object of metaphysical investigation) subverts the very possibility of ever finding such criteria. Deconstruction dislocates the understanding of identity as self-presence and offers, instead, a view of identity as difference. To the extent that identity always contains the specter of non-identity within it, the subject is always divided and identity is always purchased at the price of the exclusion of the Other, the repression or repudiation of non-identity.

Lacan, of course, provides us with a more psychoanalytic explanation of the split subject, as discussed in Chapter Two. What is significant about Lacan's theory of the constitution of the subject (the "I") in language is that it shifts the grounds of the debate away from a consideration of the identity of things in themselves towards an analysis of *identity statements*. In fact, a semiotic view of identity posits it as an effect not of essence but of language, and the "I" in language is always contingent, always provisional. The terms "contingent" and "provisional" are currently enjoying a certain vogue in poststructuralist theory, and, not insignificantly, they occur with the greatest amount of frequency in discussions on identity. These new accounts of identity often take one of two forms: they either argue that each subject is composed of multiple identities which often compete and conflict with one another, or they hold that these identities are merely political constructions and thus historically provisional and even replaceable (Penley 1986, 144–45). What worries me about these specific attempts to rethink the question of identity from a poststructuralist perspective is that difference is relocated from the space within identity to the spaces *between* identities. Difference is seen as a product of the friction between easily identifiable and unitary components of identity (sexual, racial, economic, national . . .) competing for dominance within the subject. The postmodern identity is frequently theorized as an atomic identity, fractured and disseminated into a field of dispersed energy. The appeal to metaphors drawn from modern physics is not unsuggestive: one visualizes the subject as a highly charged electronic field with multiple identity particles bouncing off each other, combining and recombining, caught in an interminable process of movement and refiguration. But such metaphors seem to me, by locating difference *outside* identity, in the spaces *between* identities, to ignore the radicality of the poststructuralist view which locates differences *within* identity. In the end, I would argue, theories of "multiple identities" fail to challenge effectively the traditional metaphysical understanding of identity as unity.[10]

The deconstruction of identity as unity poses certain vexing problems for the poststructuralist feminist. As Julia Kristeva ponders, "what can 'identity,' even 'sexual identity' mean in a new theoretical and scientific space where the very notion of identity is challenged?" ("Women's

Time" 1987, 209). Mary Ann Doane expresses a similar concern: "in an era which is post-author, post-Cartesian subject, in which the ego is seen above all as illusory in its mastery, what is the status of a search for feminine *identity*?" (1987, 9). The fear is that once we have deconstructed identity, we will have nothing (nothing, that is, which is stable and secure) upon which to base a politics. "Non-identity politics" is quickly rejected as a less than exciting and no less secure foundation upon which to organize community activism. A more appealing alternative is to shift from identity to *identities*, but such attempts to pluralize merely displace the problems surrounding questions of identity and identity politics rather than address them head on.

A more successful approach to the problem, in my mind, is that posed by Lacanian psychoanalytic critics who acknowledge that while there is no stable or uncomplicated female identity, we must nonetheless resist attempts to replace identity with something else, especially with a "new identity." The most compelling articulation of this position can be found in Jane Gallop's *The Daughter's Seduction:*

> I do not believe in some "new identity" which would be adequate and authentic. But I do not seek some sort of liberation from identity. That would lead only to another form of paralysis—the oceanic passivity of undifferentiation. Identity must be continually assumed and immediately called into question. (1982a, xii)

The deconstruction of identity, then, is not necessarily a *disavowal* of identity, as has occasionally been suggested.[11] Elaine Marks articulates the position I would like to advocate here: namely that "there must be a sense of identity, even though it would be fictitious" (1984, 110). Fictions of identity, importantly, are no less powerful for being fictions (indeed the power of fantasy marks one of Freud's most radical insights). It is not so much that we possess "contingent identities" but that identity itself is contingent: "the unconscious constantly reveals the 'failure' of identity. Because there is no continuity of psychic life, so there is no stability of sexual identity, no position for women (or for men) which is ever simply achieved." Jacqueline Rose goes on to remind us that this "failure" of identity is played out endlessly, with no promise of termination, since "there is a resistance to identity at the very heart of psychic life" ("Femininity and its Discontents" 1986, 91). Such a view of identity as unstable and potentially disruptive, as alien and incoherent, could in the end produce a more mature identity politics by militating against the tendency to erase differences and inconsistencies in the production of stable political subjects. The problem with basing political identities on identity politics is that identity politics rarely takes into account the subversive and destabilizing potential of the Unconscious. To the degree that identity is a radically *destabilizing* force and not at all a stable guarantee of a coherent politics, the current tendency to base one's politics on a rather vague and imprecise notion of identity needs to be rethought. The position I am advocating here—that an essentialist theory of identity (which sutures over the dislocating operations of the psyche) is ultimately *not* a secure foundation for politics—calls into question the view, held even by many poststructuralist feminists, that *political* identities, at least, must be secure, that the fiction of their coherency must be maintained at all costs in order for us to do our political work. It seeks to undermine the idea that politics must be steady and localizable, untroubled by psychic conflict or internal disorder—a position, I might add, which can itself easily lead to disaffection and political factiousness.

Theorizing Politics

And what of politics (the second valorized term in the conjunction identity-politics)? Politics, I would suggest, represents the aporia in much of our current political theorizing; that which signifies activism is least actively interrogated. "It does all the questioning," Bruce Robbins rightly complains, "but does not itself get questioned" (1987/88, 3). To this extent, paradoxically, politics often occupies an apolitical position in our thinking—a position of unquestioned power and privilege. We are perhaps already weary of the avalanche of papers, books, and conferences entitled "The Politics of X,"[12] and we have certainly begun to question that most hallowed of all political slogans on the left, "everything is political." But the growing discontent with the failure to historicize politics itself should not lead us on a quest to locate the "true" identity of politics. I suspect that the reason "the politics of x" formula has been in circulation so long is precisely because its "identity" has been so elusive; we do not really know what politics is (though we sometimes like to pretend its significance is self-evident). This uncertainty is embedded in the very noun "politics," which, unlike "identity," is irreducibly cast in the *plural*. That politics linguistically connotes difference, in the way identity does not, immeasurably frustrates our attempts to locate and to anatomize the identity of politics. And so, in the opinion of one influential Marxist critic, "as far as 'the political' is concerned, any single-slot, single-function definition of it is worse than misleading, it is paralyzing" (Jameson 1982, 75). Yet, what I wish to emphasize here is that the indeterminacy and confusion surrounding the sign "politics" does not typically prevent us from frequently summoning its rhetorical power to keep "theory" in its place.

For example, essentialists argue that the Foucauldian reading of sexuality as a social construct rather than a natural essence must inevitably pose a threat to a politics based on the continuity of a shared homosexual tradition. It is argued that the strict social constructionist approach "denies us a history that allows us to name Plato, Michelangelo and Sappho as our ancestors" (Gallagher and Wilson 1987, 27), and it is charged that such academic theorizing fails to speak to the lived experience and self-conceptions of most members of the gay and lesbian communities. In Steven Epstein's words, "people who base their claims to social rights on the basis of a group identity will not appreciate being told that that identity is just a social construct" (1987, 22).[13] Epstein's critique of "the limits of social constructionism" provides us with a particularly clear example of the way in which "politics" is summoned to challenge, if not to discredit, the anti-essentialist position; if such theories are to be "useful," Epstein writes, "then they should provide some means of evaluating concrete political strategies" (25). Politics is deployed as the final measuring stick for assessing the present utility, and thus the final relevance, of theories of gay identity.

But this in some ways predictable appeal to politics as a means to undercut Foucault's anti-essentialist maneuvers can never be entirely successful within the framework of Foucault's own thinking, for Foucault sees politics as a set of effects and not a first cause or final determinant.[14] To see politics as a "set of effects" rather than as the concealed motor which sets all social relations into motion would prevent us from reifying politics and mystifying its "behind-the-scenes" operations. More importantly, it would also work against the tendency in current theorizing to search for the "hidden politics" within any given text, to quest for the secret sub-text which contains the "true" intentions or "real" motivations of the writer. Such projects obscure what in my mind may be the more important question: namely, why and how is it that current critical enterprises have come to elevate politics to the status of final determinant in our theoretical debates and unquestioned authorizer of our material productions? I confess that I have become increasingly suspicious of the recurrent appeal to "political strategy" or "tactical necessity" in recent critical disputes, even though I myself have made recourse to this argument as a way to reopen feminism's case files on essentialism. My worry is that deference to the primacy and omniscience of Politics may uphold the ideology of pluralism, for no matter how reactionary or dangerous a notion may be, it can always be salvaged and kept in circulation by an appeal to "political strategy." (Indeed pluralism itself can be kept in play through an appeal to the historical urgency of its tactical deployment.) I am not suggesting that we should do away entirely with arguments of tactical necessity, but I do think that the easy recourse to political stratagem currently needs to be rethought. Perhaps the question we must always keep before us is: "politically strategic *for whom?*"

All this is not to say that the unstated political assumptions governing a given text do not deserve to be interrogated, but only that such efforts must often rely on the self-evident importance of politics, on an essentialism of the political, in order to do so. To some extent, Foucault himself, despite his initial attempts to historicize the sign of the political, is guilty of allowing politics to re-assume a certain unchallenged authority in *The History of Sexuality*. A critical suspension of the question of *sexual* politics permits Foucault to avoid confronting his own symptomatic omissions and critical oversights. Feminist theorists have rightly taken Foucault to task for his inability to account for the specificity of women's pleasure, for his refusal to engage directly with the extensive body of feminist scholarship on sexuality, for, in short, his "will not to know" about women.[15] As Teresa de Lauretis describes the problem, in Foucault's work "sexuality is not understood as gendered, as having a male form and a female form, but is taken to be one and the same for all—and consequently male" (1987, 14). These difficulties must be borne in mind as we assess the critical strengths and drawbacks of recent Foucauldian interpretations of "the homosexual role."

Inventing Homosexuality

Perhaps the greatest contribution social constructionists have made to the theory of homosexuality is their collective subversion of the traditional medical, legal, and sociological approaches to gay identities which inevitably begin with the question: is homosexuality innate or acquired? To Mary McIntosh (one of the earliest proponents of the invention theory) the debate over etiology is centered on precisely the *wrong* question: "one might as well try to trace the etiology of 'committee-chairmanship' or 'Seventh-Day Adventism' as of 'homosexuality' " (1968, 183). It is pointless to investigate the root causes of homosexuality if we realize that homosexuality is not a transhistorical, transcultural, eternal category but a socially contingent and variant construction which, according to McIntosh, did not emerge in the West until the 17th century. Though some controversy still persists over exactly which historical period first gave rise to a homosexual identity, I am inclined to agree with Barry Adam that the Western homosexual appeared along with the rise of industrial capitalism.[16] But whether the homosexual role emerged in the 17th century with the appearance of male transvestite social clubs and homosexual coteries in major cities like London (McIntosh), in the 18th century with the expansion of the wage labor sector and the growth of urban populations (Adam), or in the 19th century with the professionalization of medicine and the social organization of sexual "types" (Foucault, Weeks), the point all social constructionists agree on is that homosexuality is a comparatively late phenomenon in Western culture. This claim is asserted on the grounds that there is an important distinction to be made between "homosexual behavior, which is universal, and a homosexual identity, which is historically specific" (Weeks 1977, 3). Constructionists argue that prior to the formation of homosexual roles, there was only "same sex contact"; in order for a homosexual identity to emerge, certain historical conditions must be met, and it is these historically variable conditions, and not a stationary homosexual "type," which social constructionists take as their central object of investigation.

There are a number of critical strengths to recommend a constructionist approach to the question of homosexual identity formation and, indeed, to the subject of sexuality in general. First, invention theories, by rejecting the view of homosexuality as an eternal, culturally uniform "condition," work against the tendency to produce ethnocentric analyses of sexuality. Although the temptation to take the white, male, middle-class homosexual as the prototype for the homosexual role still persists in some constructionist work (see Faraday 1981), invention theories have the theoretical capabilities to explore the variations *among* and *within* sexual subcultures. Second, a constructionist view of homosexual identity opens the door to studies of the production of *all* sexual identities, including (and crucially) heterosexuality; for the constructionist, heterosexuality is not "natural" or "given," any more than non-hegemonic sexual classifications. Third, constructionism permits us to investigate "homosexuality," "heterosexuality," "bisexuality," and all other sexual roles precisely *as classifications*, as historically contingent categories and not transhistorical phenomena. Fourth, in addition to favoring more sophisticated analyses of how homosexual identities are socially produced, invention theories allow us to make important distinctions between male homosexuals and lesbians, two groups which are frequently conflated in the research on sexual minorities (research noticeably skewed in the direction of the gay male subject) but which, in fact, are not constructed in precisely the same ways. And finally, related to all of the above strengths, invention theories are marked by an impulse to historicize and to contextualize; such studies move us out of the realm of ontology (what the homosexual *is*) and into the realm of social and discursive formations (how the homosexual role is *produced*). For all of these reasons, social constructionism presently offers one of the strongest theoretical positions from which to broach the difficult questions of sexual identity formations and their sociopolitical inscriptions.

But the social constructionist position is not without its vulnerabilities. The most serious problem with most constructionist studies is a tendency to elide altogether the category of the psychic. This tendency usually takes one of two forms in gay theory. Either it sees psychoanalysis as a product of heterosexist hegemony and so rejects theories of psychical conflict as part of the general system of social regulation. Or it dismisses studies of "homophobia" in favor of analyses of "heterosexism."[17] This latter predilection is particularly common and especially dangerous because it fails to take into account the way in which the social interfaces with the psychic, not erases it. Simon Watney, in an otherwise brilliant critique of the ideologies of Britain's Gay Liberation Front, articulates this general distrust of the very term homophobia:

> The remarkable speed and ease with which the later concept of homophobia was taken up as an explanation of hostility towards homosexuality shows the measure of the force of the idea that sexuality is a system of innate drives rather than a range of historically and socially constructed alternatives. (1980, 68)

And Gary Kinsman, another neo-Marxist theorist, argues that the concept of homophobia "merely individualizes and privatizes gay oppression and obscures the social relations that organize it." Kinsman, like Watney, prefers the notion of "heterosexism" which connotes more accurately "the practices of heterosexual hegemony to institutional and social settings and to sex and gender relations" (1987, 29).

The problem with most emergence theory is that while it rightly insists that identities are constructions, it sees them as *social* constructions only. But to hold that there is no such thing as a natural or innate sexuality is not to abjure necessarily the category of the psychic. To jettison psychoanalysis along with essentialism (a particularly suspect move if we bear in mind that it was Freud, after all, who first challenged the "naturalness" of sexuality) is to foreclose not just the category of desire but also the question of how desire comes to be articulated within a particular social formation. In other words, it is to disregard the importance of the psychoanalytic insight which holds that homosexuality is not opposed to heterosexuality but lies within it—as its very precondition since all identity is based on exclusion. Dismissals of homophobia in favor of heterosexism overlook the fact that homosexual desire plays a role in *all* psychical identity formations.[18] Jonathan Dollimore's remarks on homophobia may offer a more reasonable solution to the problem. Homophobia, he argues, "may . . . be rooted in repressed desire. But this can't be its necessary condition since it obviously circulates without it" (1986, 10). Dollimore neither reduces gay oppression to repressed desire nor abstracts it to the level of superstructural effect; instead, he opens the door to understanding *the way in which* homophobia circulates in culture and *the mechanisms by which* heterosexism keeps it in place. Investigating the precise relation between homophobia and heterosexism strikes me as one of the most productive lines of research gay and lesbian studies might pursue in the future. In conclusion, I wish to identify two more areas which I believe represent fertile ground for gay and lesbian theory: the emergence of a lesbian/gay binarism within homosexual theory and politics, and the place of homosexuality in current theories of sexual difference.

The emergence of a lesbian/gay binarism within homosexual theory and politics. Although in current poststructuralist discussions of sameness and difference homosexuality is seen to be firmly inscribed within the conservative politics of the Same, homosexuality is obviously by no means a "homogeneous" or monolithic subject-position. And yet, theories of homosexuality, by self-identified gay and lesbian writers, do not necessarily take into account the differences among and between us. Foucault, in *The History of Sexuality,* effects a complete and total silence on the subject of lesbianism while implicitly coding homosexuality as male. And John D'Emilio, in his generally excellent historical analyses of the making of sexual communities, while certainly treating lesbianism more sympathetically than most theorists nonetheless situates lesbianism as a footnote to gay male history—the subordinated other in a newly constructed gay/lesbian binarism.[19] Several lesbian feminist theorists—Luce Irigaray, Monique Wittig, and Adrienne Rich—have in turn inverted this binarism and erected a lesbian identity on the rejection and repression of a male hom(m)o-sexual economy. In one extreme version of this view, the (male) *homosexual* is erased by feminist theorizations of the *homosocial* which posits the exchange of women between men as culture's inaugural institution of oppression.

Or, in a far more pernicious view, the homosocial is theorized as a socially acceptable expression of the homoerotic and gay men are themselves situated to bear the burden of a cultural homophobia designed to mask the determinative power of gay male relations. One needs to ask why it is that those feminist theorists (Irigaray, Wittig, Rich) who have perhaps done the most to foreground and to valorize "lesbian" in contemporary critical theory have the greatest difficulty satisfactorily accounting for male homosexuality. At the same time, one also needs to interrogate the failure on the part of those gay male theorists who have produced significant work on the question of sexuality (Foucault, D'Emilio) to theorize adequately the category "lesbian" outside the generic pretenses of "gay" or "homosexual." I believe it is imperative to begin the hard work of investigating some of these structuring tensions within the general field of gay and lesbian theory if we are to progress beyond the present state of adversarial relations where each side persistently plays out the erasure of the other.

The place of homosexuality in current theories of sexual difference. To the degree that sexual difference in poststructuralist feminist theory has long been anchored in the male/female binarism, the place accorded to homosexuality has more accurately been a no-place, or at least a no-place near the privileged space of "difference" between male and female subjects. The signification of "homo" has been linked to the politics of the phallocratic "Same," whereas the meaning of "hetero" has been associated just as insistently with the more respectable politics of "Difference." When pushed to its extreme, Derrida's conviction that "phallocentrism and homosexuality can go, so to speak, hand in hand" (1982a, 72) posits the determination of phallocentrism *within* homosexuality (here coded as male); from this perspective, heterosexuality operates as the apotheosis of "heterogeneity" and functions to displace what is perceived to be the more conservative, reactionary effects of the practice of "homogeneity." It therefore becomes important to test and to interrogate what Mandy Merck has recently identified as "the hypostatisation of heterosexual difference in contemporary theory" (1987, 6). Is there, in fact, an anti-homosexual bias in current theories of sexual difference, and if so, how has a de-privileging of the "homo" in favor of the "hetero" operated to keep these theories of sexual difference in place? What difference does homosexuality make if homosexuality is perceived as the very denial of difference? Are "homosexual," "gay," and "lesbian" themselves categories of sexual difference? Do they need the binarism of male/female in order to articulate themselves or can they be thought outside these terms? In the end, is "homosexuality" produced by, constitutive of, or situated beyond theories and categories of sexual difference?

It is important to bear in mind that all of the questions and issues I have raised above are posed in a cultural context which continues to see both homosexual men and women as a threat to public safety and indeed to state security. Recent poststructuralist theories on "the policing of desire" take on more than metaphoric significance in the context of actual legal, medical, social, and economic persecution of homosexuals by the state apparatus. Finally, then, I would like to suggest that we need to continue addressing the problem of the historical relation between the state and processes of identity formation. How does state policy (on AIDS, for example) construct, constrain, or compromise lesbian and gay activity?[20] What does it mean to be a citizen in a state which programmatically denies citizenship on the basis of sexual preference? What are the various gay and lesbian views of the state, and how does the notion that "society needs its deviants" (Dollimore 1986, 7) co-implicate gay and lesbian theory in the equally complicated processes of state formations? Do gay and lesbian subjects escape the objectification and commodification associated with the sexual marketplace, or are we, despite our many protestations to the contrary, fully inscribed within the terms of sexual exchange? These are just some of the questions which remain to be addressed fully and which might define more adequately what we mean by this new discourse of knowledge called "gay and lesbian theory."

7

Essentialism in the Classroom

No where are the related issues of essence, identity, and experience so highly charged and so deeply politicized as they are in the classroom. Personal consciousness, individual oppressions, lived experience—in short, identity politics—operate in the classroom both to authorize and to de-authorize speech. "Experience" emerges as the essential truth of the individual subject, and personal "identity" metamorphoses into knowledge. Who we are becomes what we know; ontology shades into epistemology. In this final chapter I am primarily concerned with the way in which essence circulates as a privileged signifier in the classroom, usually under the guise of "the authority of experience." Exactly what counts as "experience," and should we defer to it in pedagogical situations? Does experience of oppression confer special jurisdiction over the right to speak about that oppression? Can we only speak, ultimately, from the so-called "truth" of our experiences, or are all empirical ways of knowing analytically suspect? Finally, what is the pedagogical status of empiricism in the age of what Alice Jardine labels "the demise of Experience"? (1985, 145–55) How are we to handle our students' (and perhaps our own) daily appeals to experiential knowledge when, with the advent of poststructuralist thought, experience has been placed so convincingly under erasure?

These questions often appear particularly irresolvable and especially frustrating to the feminist scholar and teacher who has invested much of her career in the battle to validate "female experience"—in university classrooms, in academic textbooks, in curricular offerings, and even in institutional infrastructures. The category of "female experience" holds a particularly sacrosanct position in Women's Studies programs, programs which often draw on the very notion of a hitherto repressed and devalued female experience to form the basis of a new feminist epistemology. Virtually all the essays in one of the few volumes devoted entirely to questions of feminist pedagogy, *Gendered Subjects:*

The Dynamics of Feminist Teaching (Culley and Portuges 1985), uphold experience as the essential difference of the Women's Studies classroom.[1] But the problem with positing the category of experience as the basis of a feminist pedagogy is that the very object of our inquiry, "female experience," is never as unified, as knowable, as universal, and as stable as we presume it to be. This is why some feminist philosophers recommend resisting the temptation to reduce "women's experiences (plural) to women's experience (singular)" (Griffiths and Whitford 1988, 6). Certainly, Derrida is right to suggest that "egoity is the absolute form of experience" ("Violence and Metaphysics" 1978, 133), but while experience may be underwritten by a metaphysics of presence, this does not mean experience is necessarily present to us—in the form of an unmediated real. The appeal to experience, as the ultimate test of all knowledge, merely subtends the subject in its fantasy of autonomy and control. Belief in the truth of Experience is as much an ideological production as belief in the experience of Truth.

In theories of feminist pedagogy, the category of natural female experience is often held against (and posited as a corrective to) the category of imposed masculinist ideology. The experience/ideology opposition, however, simply masks the way in which experience itself is ideologically cast. One thinks immediately of Louis Althusser:

> When we speak of ideology we should know that ideology slides into all human activity, that it is identical with the "lived" experience of human existence itself. . . . This "lived" experience is not a *given*, given by a pure "reality", but the spontaneous "lived experience" of ideology in its peculiar relationship to the real. ("A Letter on Art in Reply to André Daspre" 1971, 223)

In the classical, Aristotelian view, experience is the doorway to the apprehension of essence; experience is understood as a real and immediate presence and therefore as a reliable means of knowing. In the poststructuralist, Althusserian view, experience is a product of ideology. It is a sign mediated by other signs. To Jonathan Culler, experience is fundamentally unreliable because it maintains a duplicitous standing: "it has always already occurred and yet is still to be produced—an indispensable point of reference, yet never simply there" (1982, 63). Though it is the latter view of experience which this book explicitly endorses, it is the former view, the "common-sense" Aristotelian understanding of experience, which we all carry into the classroom with us and which constitutes the grounds of a "politics of experience." While it may not always be the case that identity politics is reactionary,[2] arguments based on the authority of experience can often have surprisingly de-politicizing effects. The ideology and effects of the politics of experience are therefore particularly important to confront in the institutional classroom setting, where identities can often seem more rigidified, politics more personalized, and past histories more intensified. This final chapter is concerned with some of the unwelcome effects of essentialism in the classroom, and with the pedagogy and politics of "essentially speaking."

Problems often begin in the classroom when those "in the know" commerce only with others "in the know," excluding and marginalizing those perceived to be outside the magic circle. The circle metaphor is Edward Said's: "inside the circle stand the blameless, the just, the omnicompetent, those who know the truth about themselves as well as the others: outside the circle stand a miscellaneous bunch of querulous whining complainers" ("Intellectuals in the Post-Colonial World" 1986, 50). Said provides the most incisive and compelling critique that I know of the phenomenon which I sometimes call "inside trading." (The economic metaphor is, of course, a calculated one; in the classroom identities are nothing if not commodities.) For Said it is both dangerous and misleading to base an identity politics upon rigid theories of exclusions, "exclusions that stipulate, for instance, only women can understand feminine experience, only Jews can understand Jewish suffering, only formerly colonial subjects can understand colonial experience" (55). The artificial boundary between insider and outsider necessarily contains rather than disseminates knowledge:

> the difficulties with theories of exclusiveness or with barriers and sides is that once admitted these polarities absolve and forgive a great deal more ignorance and demagogy than they enable knowledge. . . . If you know in advance that the black or Jewish or German experience is fundamentally comprehensible only to Jews or Blacks or Germans you first of all posit as essential something which, I believe, is both historical and the result of interpretation—namely the existence of Jewishness, Blackness, or Germanness, or for that matter of Orientalism and Occidentalism. Secondly you are pretty likely to construct defenses of the experience rather than promote knowledge of it. And, as a result, you will demote the different experience of others to a lesser status. (55–56)

Experience, then, while providing some students with a platform from which to speak can also relegate other students to the sidelines. Exclusions of this sort often breed exclusivity.

The politics of experience sometimes takes the form of a tendency amongst both individuals and groups to "one down" each other on the oppression scale. Identities are itemized, appreciated, and ranked on the basis of which identity holds the greatest currency at a particular historical moment and in a particular institutional setting. Thus, in an Afro-American Studies classroom, race and ethnicity are likely to emerge as the privileged items of intellectual exchange, or, in a Gay Studies classroom, sexual "preference" may hold the top notch on the scale of oppressions. This delimiting of boundaries or mapping out of critical terrains is not a problem in and of itself (especially if it allows us to devote serious attention to previously ignored or trivialized issues); however, it becomes a problem when the central category of difference under consideration blinds us to other modes of difference and implicitly delegitimates them. Let me pose an example. Recently a student in a class on postcolonialism objected to another student's interest in the social and structural forms of non-Western homosexual relations; "what on earth does sexual preference have to do with imperialism?" the angry student charged. The class as a whole had no immediate response to the indictment and so we returned to the "real" issue at hand (race and ethnicity); the gay student was effectively silenced. Another common version of this phenomenon is the synecdochical tendency to see only one part of a subject's identity (usually the most visible part) and to make that part stand for the whole. A male professor, for example, is typically reduced to his "maleness," an Asian professor to his or her "Asianness," a lesbian professor to her "lesbianness," and so on. A hierarchy of identities is set up *within* each speaking subject (not just between subjects), and it is this ranking of identities which is often used either to authorize an individual to speak on the basis of the truth of her lived experience (as in the case of a female professor in a Women's Studies classroom) or to de-authorize an individual from speaking on the basis of his *lack* of experience (as in the case of a male professor in a Women's Studies classroom). Identities are treated as fixed, accessible, and determinative, conferring upon the subject's speech an aura of predictability ("Male professors *always* say such things" or "*No* Third World writer would ever make such a claim" are often common refrains). What we see in this ordering of identities is none other than the paradoxical and questionable assumption that some essences are more *essential* than others.

It is the unspoken law of the classroom not to trust those who cannot cite experience as the indisputable grounds of their knowledge. Such unwritten laws pose perhaps the most serious threat to classroom dynamics in that they breed suspicion amongst those inside the circle

[margin note: Synecdochical - part stands for whole]

[margin note: hierarchy of identities within each speaking subject]

and guilt (sometimes anger) amongst those outside the circle. In its most extreme incarnation, the guilt of the outsiders is exploited by the insiders to keep everyone in line—that is, to regulate and to police group behavior. "Provoking guilt is a tactic not so much for informing as it is for controlling others," Anne Koedt has written in challenging the notion of "lesbians-as-the-vanguard-of-feminism" ("Lesbianism and Feminism," Koedt et al. 1973, 256). When provoking guilt in "the enemy" becomes the prime motivation for one's politics, we have to begin to question what negative effects such a project might possibly have, especially in the classroom. The tendency to psychologize and to personalize questions of oppression, *at the expense of* strong materialist analyses of the structural and institutional bases of exploitation, poses one such undesirable effect. As we have seen, contrary to the well-worn feminist dictum, "the personal is political," personalizing exploitation can often amount to de-politicizing it:

> Power then becomes primarily a personal issue between individuals—men and women, white and black, gentile and Jew, heterosexual and gay—and not the way an exploitative system is hierarchically structured so as to get maximum differentiation. (Bourne 1987, 14)

We have to be willing to acknowledge, along with Simon Watney, that "the politics of provocation are comprehensible only to the provocateurs" (1980, 72). We have to be willing to recognize that when identity politics is used to monitor who can and cannot speak in the classroom, its effects can be counterproductive. Rather than automatically interjecting a political note, arguments based on the authority of experience can just as often be radically de-politicizing.

Though I remain convinced that appeals to the authority of experience rarely advance discussion and frequently provoke confusion (I am always struck by the way in which introjections of experiential truths into classroom debates dead-end the discussion), I also remain wary of any attempts to prohibit the introduction of personal histories into such discussions on the grounds that they have yet to be adequately "theorized." The anti-essentialist displacement of experience must not be used as a convenient means of silencing students, no matter how shaky experience has proven to be as a basis of epistemology. It is certainly true that there is no such thing as "the female experience" or "the Black experience" or "the Jewish experience". . . . And it seems likely that simply *being* a woman, or a Black, or a Jew (as if "being" were ever "simple") is not enough to qualify one as an official spokesperson for an entire community. But while truth clearly does not equate with experience, it cannot be denied that it is precisely the fiction that they *are* the same which prompts many students, who would not perhaps speak otherwise, to enter energetically into those debates they perceive as pertaining directly to them. The authority of experience, in other words, not only works to silence students, it also works to empower them. How are we to negotiate the gap between the conservative fiction of experience as the ground of all truth-knowledge and the immense power of this fiction to enable and encourage student participation?

While experience can never be a reliable guide to the real, this is not to preclude any role at all for experience in the realm of knowledge production. If experience is itself a product of ideological practices, as Althusser insists, then perhaps it might function as a window onto the complicated workings of ideology. Experience would itself then become "evidence" of a sort for the productions of ideology, but evidence which is obviously constructed and clearly knowledge-dependent. What I mean by this is simply that experience is not the raw material knowledge seeks to understand, but rather knowledge is the active process which produces its own objects of investigation, including empirical facts. The theory of experience I have in mind here is, of course, a constructionist one, and is articulated best by two post-Althusserians, Barry Hindess and Paul Hirst:

> Empiricism represents knowledge as constructed out of 'given' elements, the elements of experience, the 'facts' of history, etc. Unfortunately for these positions facts are never 'given' to knowledge. They are always the product of definite practices, theoretical or ideological, conducted under definite real conditions. . . . Facts are never *given;* they are always produced. (1975, 2–3)

The idea that empirical facts are always ideological productions can itself be a useful fact to introduce to students. And, in terms of pedagogical theory, such a position permits the introduction of narratives of lived experience into the classroom while at the same time challenging us to examine collectively the central role social and historical practices play in shaping and producing these narratives. "Essentially speaking," we need both to theorize essentialist spaces from which to speak and, simultaneously, to deconstruct these spaces to keep them from solidifying. Such a double gesture involves once again the responsibility to historicize, to examine each deployment of essence, each appeal to experience, each claim to identity in the complicated contextual frame in which it is made.

It may well be that the best way to counteract the negative, often hidden effects of essentialism in the classroom is to bring essentialism to the fore as an explicit topic of debate. This book aims to contribute to the renewed interest in rethinking essentialism by laying out the terms of the essentialist/constructionist opposition while also providing the critical lever to displace what, in my mind, is a largely artificial (albeit powerful) antagonism. I have argued from the start that essentialism underwrites theories of constructionism and that construction- ism operates as a more sophisticated form of essentialism. This is simply another way of saying that constructionism may be more normative, and essentialism more variable, than those of us who call ourselves poststructuralists hitherto have been willing to acknowledge. Any attempt to intervene in the stalemate produced by the essentialist/ constructionist stand-off must therefore involve a recognition of each position's internal contradictions and political investments. While the essentialist/constructionist polemic may continue to cast its shadow over our critical discussions, it is the final contention of this book that reliance on an admittedly overvalued binarism need not be paralyzing.

Notes

Introduction

1 Stephen Heath (1978), Alice Jardine (1987), Naomi Schor (1987), and Gayatri Spivak (1987) have all endorsed a renewed consideration of essentialism.

2 Teresa de Lauretis, for example, has at different times articulated both these positions. See "Feminist Studies/Critical Studies: Issues, Terms, and Contexts," in *Feminist Studies/Critical Studies* (1986, 2) and *The Technologies of Gender: Essays on Theory, Film, and Fiction* (1987, 10).

1 The "Risk" of Essence

1 A comprehensive discussion of the essence/accident distinction is elaborated in Book Z of Aristotle's *Metaphysics*. For a history of the philosophical concept of essentialism, readers might wish to consult DeGrood (1976) or Rorty (1979).

2 See, for example, Hélène Cixous's contribution to *The Newly Born Woman* (1986).

3 I want to emphasize here that most feminist theorists are, in fact, *both* essentialists and constructionists. E. Ann Kaplan, who often takes the essentialist/anti-essentialist distinction as a primary organizational frame in her discussions of film and television criticism, has identified four "types" of feminism: bourgeois feminism, Marxist feminism, radical feminism, and poststructuralist feminism (1987, 216). The first three types—bourgeois, Marxist, and radical—Kaplan categorizes under the rubric "essentialist"; the fourth type—poststructuralist—she labels "anti-essentialist." I would submit that the division here is much too simplistic to be useful: it sees *all* poststructuralist feminists as anti-essentialists and *all other* feminists as essentialists. Such a schema cannot adequately account, for example, for the work of Luce Irigaray, a poststructuralist Derridean who many consider to be an essentialist; nor can it account for a theorist like Monique Wittig who appears to fall into at least two of Kaplan's essentialist categories, Marxist feminism and radical feminism, and yet who identifies herself as a committed social constructionist. We must be extremely wary of using the constructionist/essentialist opposition as a taxonomic device for elaborating oversimplified and deceptive typologies (another powerful argument to be made in favor of working to subvert, rather than to reify, this particularly pervasive dualism).

4   I am reminded of that curious but common saying, "second nature." The qualifier "second" implies orders, gradations, types of "nature." It further implies that some "kinds" of nature may be closer to the ideal or prototype than others—indeed, that some may be more "natural" than others. Essentialism here crumbles under the weight of its own self-contradiction and opens the door to viewing essence as a social construct, a production of language.

5   For example, the nominal essence of gold (Locke's favorite example) would be "that complex idea the word gold stands for, let it be, for instance a body yellow, of a certain weight, malleable, fusible, and fixed"; its real essence would be "the constitution of the insensible parts of that body, on which those qualities, and all the other properties of gold depend" (Locke 1690, 13.6). Locke discusses real versus nominal essence in numerous passages of *An Essay Concerning Human Understanding*, the most important of which are 2.31; 3.3; 3.6; 3.10; 4.6; and 4.12.

6   Currently, the subjects of agency, change, and determination are beginning to receive more careful consideration, especially from social constructionists. In my mind, one of the most impressive attempts to come to grips with this difficult series of problems is Paul Smith's *Discerning the Subject* (1988).

7   See "Così Fan Tutti" in Irigaray 1977a, and "Le Facteur de la Vérité" in Derrida 1980.

8   See MacCannell 1986, chapter one, and Ragland-Sullivan 1986, chapter five.

9   As we might expect, Derrida criticizes Lacan's adherence to the metaphysical privilege accorded to speech over writing. Idealism, Derrida argues, is lodged in Lacan's emphasis on *logos as phonē*, on the truth of the spoken word, on the privileging of voice and the vocalizable (see "Le Facteur de la Vérité" 1980, 413–96).

10 Benvenuto and Kennedy (1986, 10). These writers are correct to point out that most if not all psychoanalysts presume to have access to the "real" Freud; however, in a project as rigorously anti-essentialist as Lacan's, the retention of this mythology of the true Freud cannot be so easily dismissed—it must be *explained*.

11 Other early interrogations of phenomenology can be found in Derrida's introduction to Husserl's *L'Origine de la géométrie* (1962); "Form and Meaning: A Note on the Phenomenology of Language" (1972b); and "'Genesis and Structure' and Phenomenology" (1967c).

12 Derrida also provides a particularly incisive critique of Husserl's theory of signs. As a science, phenomenology is blind to its own medium, its own status as discourse; what is self-evident in Husserl's work, and therefore outside the realm of his phenomenological investigation, is precisely the materiality of language and the historicity of the sign.

13 Though we have come to associate this phrase with Derrida, it has, in fact, a more extended philosophical history. One can detect its recurrence in the works of such disparate theorists as Husserl, Heidegger, Althusser, and Lacan. For Derrida's discussion of Heidegger's use of "always already," see "The Ends of Man," 1972b, 124–25.

14 Toril Moi's *Sexual/Textual Politics* provides a particularly good example of how this locution can be used to dismiss entire schools of feminist thought—in Moi's case, to discredit "Anglo-American" feminism. Moi's sweeping criticism of writers

as diverse as Elaine Showalter, Myra Jehlen, Annette Kolodny, Sandra Gilbert, and Susan Gubar consists mainly in mapping out in detail the points in which their analyses "slip into" essentialism and therefore "reinscribe patriarchal humanism." Such an ostensibly anti-essentialist critique can only be built on the grounds of the twin assumptions that essentialism is, in essence, "patriarchal" and that "patriarchal humanism" has an essence which is inherently, inevitably reactionary.

2 Reading Like a Feminist

1 For Scholes's project to "save the referent," see "Reference and Difference" in *Textual Power: Literary Theory and the Teaching of English* (86–110).

2 See Paul Smith, "Men in Feminism: Men and Feminist Theory" (33–40); Stephen Heath, "Men in Feminism: Men and Feminist Theory" (41–46); Cary Nelson, "Men, Feminism: The Materiality of Discourse" (153–72); and Rosi Braidotti, "Envy: or With My Brains and Your Looks" (233–41), all in Jardine and Smith (1987).

3 For a more detailed reading of the constitution of the sexed subject, see Lacan's "The Mirror Stage" in *Écrits* (1–7).

4 For a summary statement of the collective's theoretical positions, see Guha (1984, vii–viii).

5 For this critique of essentialism in the Subaltern Studies group, see especially pp. 202–207.

6 The phrase is Naomi Schor's: "what is it to say that the discourse of sexual indifference/pure difference is not the last or (less triumphantly) the latest ruse of phallocentrism?" (1987, 109). This is implicitly a critique of Foucault's *anti*-essentialism, suggesting that both essentialism and anti-essentialism can have reactionary effects.

7 Schor's helpful definition of "reading double" as reading both for and beyond difference can be found in "Reading Double: Sand's Difference" (1986b, 250).

8 Spivak insists hers is merely a reading strategy and not a comprehensive theory. The distinction she makes between these two notions is not entirely clear: is it possible to employ a reading strategy *outside* a larger theoretical framework?

3 Monique Wittig's Anti-essentialist Materialism

1 I am reminded of Muhammed Ali's comment on the ERA: "some professions shouldn't be open to women because they can't handle certain jobs, like construction work. Lesbians, maybe, but not women." Cited in Alice Walker's "Breaking Chains and Encouraging Life" (1983, 287).

2 Chodorow does make the point that most women are heterosexual because the development of industrial capitalism has made primary relationships with women "rare" and "turned women (and men) increasingly and exclusively to conjugal family relationships for emotional support and love" (200). This thinking stands in sharp contradiction to recent gay theory which holds that it is precisely industrial capitalism which creates the new social and sexual relations necessary for the formation of a gay or lesbian identity. I will return to this important point in Chapter Six.

3 As Eve Sedgwick accurately assesses the problem, "the male homosexuality discussed . . . turns out to represent anything but actual sex between men" (1985, 26). For another particularly incisive critique of Irigaray's theory of hom(m)o-sexuality, see Craig Owens's "Outlaws: Gay Men in Feminism," in Jardine and Smith (1987, 219–32).

4 Denise Riley's *War in the Nursery* posed many of these important questions several years ago (see especially chapter one), but unfortunately this fascinating text has not yet received the serious critical attention it deserves.

4 Luce Irigaray's Language of Essence

1 Two earlier introductory pieces to French feminist theory also appear in *Signs:* see Marks (1978) and Burke (1978).

2 For another sympathetic reading of Irigaray, and an application of her deconstructive feminism, see Féral (1981). I did not have the pleasure of reading Naomi Schor's excellent piece, "This Essentialism Which Is Not One: Coming to Grips With Irigaray" (1989) before completing this chapter. Schor's article is, among other things, an important reminder that Irigaray's philosophical corpus extends beyond the publication of *Ce Sexe qui n'en est pas un.* One can only lament the translation industry's slowness in keeping up with Irigaray's productive output as compared, for example, to the many excellent and timely translations of the work of one of her male contemporaries, Jacques Derrida.

3 Irigaray makes a distinction between "morphological" and "anatomical" in "Women's Exile" (1977b, 64), but I agree with both Monique Plaza (1978, 31) and Toril Moi (1985, 143) that the distinction is too imprecise to be helpful.

4 Carolyn Burke makes a similar argument in defense of Irigaray: to reduce "the subtlety of Irigaray's thought to a simple argument 'from the body,' in order to then point out that such arguments are, indeed, essentialist" amounts to a circular argument based on a rather questionable initial reading (1981, 302).

5 Vincent Leitch writes that, by the early 1980s, Derrida had formulated more than three dozen such substitutions (see Leitch 1983, 43).

6 For a recent rereading and application of Jakobson's terms, see Johnson (1984, 205–19).

7 Studies of metaphor have also dominated over studies of metonymy in the comparatively recent history of linguistic and semiotic research. Jakobson explains: "Similarity in meaning connects the symbols of a metalanguage with the symbols of the language referred to. Similarity connects a metaphorical term with the term for which it is substituted. Consequently, when constructing a metalanguage to interpret tropes, the researcher possesses more homogeneous means to handle metaphor, whereas metonymy, based on a different principle, easily defies interpretation. Therefore nothing comparable to the rich literature on metaphor can be cited for the theory of metonymy" (1956, 81).

8 Jane Gallops' *Reading Lacan* (1985) also addresses the penis/phallus distinction, focusing specifically on the linguistic sources of the confusion. See especially chapter 6, "Reading the Phallus," pp. 133–156. See also Gallop's "Phallus/Penis: Same Difference" in *Men by Women*, Vol. 2 of *Women and Literature* (1981).

9   The reference is to Freud's "Constructions in Analysis" (1937): "I have not been able to resist the seduction of an analogy." Jane Gallop has cleverly suggested that Irigaray's general resistance to analogical reasoning is based on a more specific repudiation of Freud's anal-logical model of sexual difference. Irigaray's refusal of analogy can thus be read within the wider frame of a deep skepticism concerning the anal fixation of Freud's own theories (see Gallop 1982a, 68–69).

10 See also Plaza (1978) and Adams and Brown (1979).

11 Naomi Schor has made a similar point which I find compelling: "in both Cixous and Irigaray the anti-essentialist aspect of their work is that which is most derivative, that is most Derridean. When Cixous and Irigaray cease to mime the master's voice and speak in their own voices, they speak a dialect of essentialese, the language of what they construe as the feminine, and wishing it weren't so won't make it go away. Rather than simply wanting to excise this unsightly excrescence, I think it would be ultimately more interesting and surely more difficult to attempt to understand just how and why a Cixous and an Irigaray deconstruct and construct femininity at the same time" (see Schor 1986a, 98–99).

12 Most of Irigaray's remarks on Aristotle can be found in the chapter entitled "How to Conceive (of) a Girl" in *Speculum*, pp. 160–67. For Aristotle's own comments on essence, see especially *Categories, Physics, Metaphysics*, and *On the Generation of Animals*, all of which can be found in McKeon 1941.

13 For Lacan's distinction between being and having the phallus, see "The Meaning of the Phallus" in Mitchell and Rose 1982, esp. 82–84. Both girl and boy are the phallus in the pre-oedipal stage; that is, both are the phallus *for* the mother. But during the crucial ascension to sexual difference through the recognition and representation of lack (the castration complex) the possession of a penis allows the boy to *have* the phallus while the girl continues to *be* it. For Lacan, it is this distinction between being and having the phallus which facilitates the taking on of a sexed subject position, the production of masculine or feminine subjects.

5   Poststructuralist Afro-American Literary Theory

1   The articles in *"Race," Writing, and Difference* are culled from a special issue of *Critical Inquiry* by the same title, 12:1 (Autumn 1985), and the responses to this issue included in 13:1 (Autumn 1986). My own pagination will follow the original *Critical Inquiry* volumes.

2   The syntax makes it clear here that it is not race which (pre)determines immoral behavior but rather immoral behavior which determines racial identity. In Fanon's opinion, one formulation is as racist as the other.

3   See also Cavalli-Sforza (1974).

4   See Johnson 1980. Although an analytic philosopher, Appiah frequently employs classic deconstructionist moves such as this one in order to advance an argument (suggesting a far less denigrated role for Continental philosophy than most analytic philosophers are willing to allow).

5   See Harvey (1986, ix–xiii) for a brief but lucid discussion on the contradictory reception of Derrida's work in the humanities.

6   Gates refers to "the Naipaul fallacy" in both "Criticism in the Jungle" (1984, 16–17) and "Writing 'Race' and the Difference It Makes" (1985, 14–15).

7   Derrida repeatedly comes back to the problem of translation in his work; it emerges as a central focus in a number of earlier essays, including "Freud and the Scene of Writing" in *Writing and Difference* (1967c); "Fors" (1977); "Me—Psychoanalysis: An Introduction to 'The Shell and the Kernel' by Nicolas Abraham" (1979b); "Living On: Borderlines" (1979a); and "Du Tout" in *The Post Card* (1980).

8   This article has been reprinted in Gates's recent collection of essays, *Figures in Black: Words, Signs, and the "Racial" Self* (1987, 235–76).

9   Abrahams (1970, 53). Gates takes this saying as one of his epigraphs.

10 A study of "woman-as-sign in semiotic systems" is rejected by Showalter in her dismissal of something she calls "feminist reading" or "feminist critique," a mode of interpretation deemed "invigorating" and "influential" but nonetheless too "ideological" and too "pluralistic" to be truly useful. See "Feminist Criticism in the Wilderness" (12–13). Showalter seems to have substantially revised her position on semiotics since this seminal piece first appeared in *Critical Inquiry*. A later article in *Raritan* (Fall 1983) cleverly decodes the operation of the sign "woman" in the work of several influential male critics. See "Critical Cross-Dressing: Male Feminists and the Woman of the Year." Reprinted in Jardine and Smith (1987, 116–32).

11 This essay originally appeared in *Black American Literature Forum* (Winter 1981), but was revised for inclusion as chapter two in *Blues, Ideology, and Afro-American Literature: A Vernacular Theory* (1984). I will be citing from this revised version.

12 Henry Louis Gates, Jr. has also recently identified four dominant critical practices that map the development of Afro-American criticism: "the Black Aesthetic" (cultural nationalism), "Repetition and Imitation" (formalism, structuralism), "Repetition and Difference" (poststructuralism) and "Synthesis" (the black vernacular). By "Synthesis" Gates seems to have in mind not a Hegelian notion of incorporation but rather a blues notion of improvisation. Thus Gates's role as critical "synthesizer" and Baker's self-defined position as "blues critic" are closely aligned: "what I have attempted to do with literary theory," Gates explains, "is modelled on what blues and jazz musicians do with received musical conventions." See Gates (1987a, xxv–xxx).

13 Baker develops his theory of "trance" in chapter three of *Afro-American Poetics: Revisions of Harlem and the Black Aesthetic* (1988).

14 See Peggy Kamuf's "Replacing Feminist Criticism" and Nancy K. Miller's "The Text's Heroine: A Feminist Critic and Her Fictions" in *Diacritics* 12 (Summer 1982). See also Peggy Kamuf's "Writing Like a Woman" (1980).

15 See Omi and Winant, especially chapter four. Omi and Winant's Gramscian-based theory of racial formation deserves particular attention.

16 For a thorough discussion of ethnicity, see Petersen (1980).

17 For an example of Hogue's own materialist literary criticism, see "History, the Feminist Discourse, and Alice Walker's *The Third Life of Grange Copeland*," in *MELUS* 12:2 (Summer 1985).

18 References to discourse theory appear with some regularity in poststructuralist Afro-American literary theory. Foucault's theory of discursive formations and the "archaeology of knowledge" has influenced both Baker and Hogue in their attempts

to formulate an Afro-American materialist criticism. Craig Werner's theory of "geneological criticism" is also clearly indebted to Foucault (see Werner 1986).

19 Two noteworthy exceptions in Afro-American criticism are Roger J. Bresnahan's "The Implied Readers of Booker T. Washington's Autobiographies" (1980) and Jerry W. Ward's "The Black Critic as Reader" (1980).

20 Carby's *Reconstructing Womanhood* is especially rigorous in its insistence on the need to de-essentialize black feminist criticism: "a black feminist criticism cannot afford to be essentialist and ahistorical, reducing the experience of all black women to a common denominator and limiting black feminist critics to an exposition of an equivalent black 'female imagination' " (1987, 10).

21 A fascinating move in this direction is Hortense Spillers's "Mama's Baby, Papa's Maybe" (1987) in which she theorizes, in effect, an *anti-Symbolic*. Stripped under slavery of his patronymic privilege, the Afro-American male is materially dispossessed and doubly castrated; the Name-of-the-Father is culturally displaced to the Law-of-the-Mother.

6   The Question of Identity Politics

1   This is the title of an important collection of essays, edited by Kenneth Plummer (1981), which explores the social construction of homosexuality in Western culture.

2   Luce Irigaray is perhaps the best example of this tendency (see Chapter Four).

3   The work of several French lesbian materialists mark an important exception to this general rule: Christine Delphy, Monique Plaza, and, of course, Monique Wittig all offer anti-essentialist approaches to the lesbian subject. For further growing feminist interest in the social construction of lesbianism, see Ferguson (1981) and Lesselier (1987).

4   The statement itself dates from April 1977.

5   From an unpublished paper by Smith, cited in Moraga (131).

6   This argument has also been forcefully articulated by Elshstain (1983, 267–69) and Adams and Minson (1978, 57). For a critique of "coming out" as the cornerstone of a gay identity politics, see Minson (1981).

7   On the question of essentialism, Bourne both goes too far in her critique of identity politics and simultaneously not far enough. She goes too far when she insists that all attentions paid to the personal (to "oppression") are essentially, necessarily de-politicizing (is the bar between oppression/exploitation really so solid and impermeable?). And she doesn't go far enough when she rightly objects to a failure in much feminist theory to account for the categories of the material and the social but does not herself historicize or contextualize the notions of "identity," "politics," and "identity politics" (under what historical conditions and for what specific groups might an adherence to identity politics *not* signify a "stunted" or "self-righteous" politics?).

8   See Munitz (1971) for a series of analytical investigations into the problem of identity.

9   A representative example would be Brody (1980).

10 Martin Heidegger's *Identity and Difference* (1957) provides us with a way to conceptualize identity outside unity, and offers us a theory of identity which undoes

the binary logic in Aristotle that opposes identity to difference. The conventional logical script for representing the principle of identity is the formula "A = A," but as Heidegger points out, "for something to be the same, one is always enough. Two are not needed" (23–24). The doubling of this logical equation demonstrates how sameness always contains difference within it: "sameness implies the relation of 'with,' that is, a mediation, a connection, a synthesis: the unification into a unity. This is why throughout the history of Western thought identity appears as unity" (25). The important word here is "appears": identity only appears as unity, but contains difference within it as the very predicate of its fictional coherence (A = A). In this respect it would perhaps not be inappropriate to revise the title of Heidegger's *Identity and Difference* to the more apt *Identity as Difference*.

11 See, for example, the introduction to *Re-vision: Essays in Feminist Film Criticism* in which the editors remark that "Irigaray points to a very real tendency in much contemporary feminist theory—a tendency to deconstruct and disavow all notions of identity, ownership, possession" (Doane et al. 1984, 10).

12 Bruce Robbins's "The Politics of Theory" is one such piece which, in a self-reflexive parody of its own title, asks whether "the 'politics of x' formula lends itself to self-flattery and hazy thinking" (3).

13 Epstein's approach to the question of identity politics in "Gay Politics, Ethnic Identity: The Limits of Social Constructionism" provides an important and useful overview of the history of social constructionism in gay theory. Where our accounts most radically differ is on the question of identity; while Epstein bases his working definition of identity on ego psychology and object-relations theory, my own work advocates a more poststructuralist view.

14 Foucault, in fact, tends to use *theory* to keep *politics* in line: "I have never tried to analyze anything whatsoever from the point of view of politics, but always to ask politics what it had to say about the problems with which it was confronted. I question it about the positions it takes and the reasons it gives for this; I don't ask it to determine the theory of what I do" ("Polemics, Politics, and Problemizations," 385). In another interview on politics, Foucault also makes the point (as if in anticipation of the current, highly sensationalized controversy over Paul de Man's early journalism) that "the 'best' theories do not constitute a very effective protection against disastrous political choices" ("Politics and Ethics: An Interview," 374). Both interviews can be found in *The Foucault Reader* (1984).

15 See Martin (1982), Schor (1987), and Plaza (1981).

16 Adam argues, in brief, that the transition to capitalism produced the structural conditions necessary for the development of new forms of identity; with the move to the cities and the subsequent dissolution of the agrarian family unit, traditional kinship ties were loosened, permitting the emergence of different sets of social and personal relations (see Adam 1985).

17 Kenneth Plummer's influential work on "Homosexual Categories" appears to be largely responsible for the general trend in gay and lesbian theory to dismiss psychoanalytic studies of homophobia in favor of social science analyses of heterosexism (see Plummer 1981, 53–75). Social constructionist theory in general is heavily weighted towards the social sciences, contributing to the tendency amongst researchers to bracket questions of desire, fantasy, and the unconscious and to emphasize instead sociality, institutions, and ideology. *The Making of the Modern*

Homosexual, edited by Plummer (1981), is a prime example of the strengths and weaknesses of such an approach.

18 This is the main import of Freud's "Psychogenesis of a Case of Homosexuality in a Woman" (1920).

19 D'Emilio, along with other historians of gay culture (Bullough, Katz), do indeed discuss lesbianism in their works (and for this they are to be commended), but they tend to confine their substantive comments on the subject of gay women to a separate chapter, thereby structurally reinforcing the impression that lesbian identity is a variant or a sub-classification of male homosexuality. Jeffrey Weeks's Foucauldian work on sexuality marks an important exception to this tendency to insert the lesbian subject into gay male paradigms (see Weeks 1979, 1985, 1986).

20 The recent investigations into the cultural representations of AIDS fall largely under this category. Simon Watney's *Policing Desire: Pornography, AIDS and the Media* (1987) and the special issue on AIDS in *October* 43 (Winter 1987) are exemplary analyses of the social construction of AIDS and the determinative role of the state in legislating, monitoring, and producing sexual desire.

7   Essentialism in the Classroom

1 See especially Frances Maher's "Classroom Pedagogy and the New Scholarship on Women," and Janet Rifkin's "Teaching Mediation: A Feminist Perspective on the Study of Law." Maher calls for new "appropriate teaching styles to recover the female experience" since "the dominant pedagogical style of most classrooms discriminate against women's experience" (29 and 31), and Janet Rifkin echoes the call for "a pedagogy in which personal experience is viewed as a legitimate and important reference-point for scholarly work" (104).

2 I am here taking issue with a prevalent strain of feminist poststructuralist thinking, represented by Jane Gallop, which holds that "the politics of experience is inevitably a conservative politics" (1983, 83). Could we not rephrase this question to read: "*In my experience,* the politics of experience is inevitably a conservative politics"?

Bibliography

Abel, Elizabeth (ed). 1982. *Writing and Sexual Difference*. Chicago: University of Chicago Press.

Abrahams, Roger D. 1970. *Deep Down in the Jungle . . . : Negro Narrative Folklore From the Streets of Philadelphia*. Chicago: Aldine.

Adam, Barry. 1985. "Structural Foundations of the Gay World." *Comparative Study of Society and History* 27:4 (October): 658–71.

Adams, Parveen and Beverly Brown. 1979. "The Feminine Body and Feminist Politics." *m/f* 3: 35–50.

Adams, Parveen and Jeff Minson. 1978. "The 'Subject' of Feminism." *m/f* 2: 43–61.

Althusser, Louis. 1971. *Lenin and Philosophy*. Trans. Ben Brewster. New York and London: Monthly Review Press.

Anozie, Sunday O. 1981. *Structural Models and African Poetics: Towards a Paradigmatic Theory of Literature*. London: Routledge & Kegan Paul.

Appiah, Anthony. 1984. "Strictures on Structures: The Prospects for a Structuralist Poetics of African Fiction." In Gates 1984, 127–50.

Appiah, Anthony. 1985. "The Uncompleted Argument: DuBois and the Illusion of Race." *Critical Inquiry* 12:1 (Autumn): 21–37.

Baker, Houston A., Jr., 1981. "Generational Shifts and the Recent Criticism of Afro-American Literature." *Black American Literature Forum* (Winter): 3–21.

Baker, Houston A., Jr., 1984. *Blues, Ideology, and Afro-American Literature: A Vernacular Theory*. Chicago: University of Chicago Press.

Baker, Houston A., Jr. 1986. "Caliban's Triple Play." *Critical Inquiry* 13:1 (Autumn): 182–96.

Baker, Houston A., Jr. 1987. "In Dubious Battle." *New Literary History* 18:2 (Winter): 363–69.

Baker, Houston A., Jr. 1988. *Afro-American Poetics: Revisions of Harlem and the Black Aesthetic*. Madison: University of Wisconsin Press.

Barthes, Roland. 1957. *Mythologies*. Paris: Editions du Seuil. Trans. Annette Lavers (1972). New York: Hill and Wang.

Benvenuto, Bice and Roger Kennedy. 1986. *The Works of Jacques Lacan*. New York: St. Martin's Press.

Bourne, Jenny. 1987. "Homelands of the Mind: Jewish Feminism and Identity Politics." *Race & Class* 29:1 (Summer): 1–24.

Boyers, Robert and George Steiner (eds). 1983. *Homosexuality: Sacrilege, Vision, Politics.* Saratoga Springs: Skidmore College.

Bresnahan, Roger J. 1980. "The Implied Readers of Booker T. Washington's Autobiographies." *Black American Literature Forum* 14:1 (1980): 15–20.

Brody, Baruch A. 1980. *Identity and Essence.* Princeton: Princeton University Press.

Bullough, Vern L. 1979. *Homosexuality: A History.* New York: New American Library.

Burke, Carolyn. 1978. "Report from Paris: Women's Writing and the Women's Movement." *Signs* 3:4 (Summer): 843–55.

Burke, Carolyn. 1981. "Irigaray Through the Looking Glass." *Feminist Studies* 7:2 (Summer): 288–306.

Carby, Hazel V. 1987. *Reconstructing Womanhood: The Emergence of the Afro-American Woman Novelist.* New York: Oxford University Press.

Cavalli-Sforza, L. L. 1974. "The Genetics of Human Populations." *Scientific American* (September): 81–9.

Chodorow, Nancy. 1978. *The Reproduction of Mothering: Psychoanalysis and the Sociology of Gender.* Berkeley: University of California Press.

Christian, Barbara. 1988. "The Race for Theory." *Feminist Studies* 14:1 (Spring): 67–79.

Cixous, Hélène and Catherine Clément. 1975. *La jeune neé.* Paris: Union Générale d'Editions. Trans. Betsy Wing (1986). *The Newly Born Woman.* Minneapolis: University of Minnesota Press.

Combahee River Collective. 1982. "A Black Feminist Statement." In Gloria T. Hull, Patricia Bell Scott, and Barbara Smith (eds). *All the Women Are White, All the Blacks Are Men, But Some of Us Are Brave: Black Women's Studies.* Old Westbury, NY: The Feminist Press.

Coward, Rosalind. 1983. *Patriarchal Precedents: Sexuality and Social Relations.* London: Routledge & Kegan Paul.

Crimp, Douglas, (ed.) Special issue on AIDS. *October 43* (Winter 1987).

Culler, Jonathan. 1982. *On Deconstruction: Theory and Criticism after Structuralism.* Ithaca: Cornell University Press.

Culley, Margo and Catherine Portuges (eds). 1985. *Gendered Subjects: The Dynamics of Feminist Teaching.* Boston: Routledge & Kegan Paul.

DeGrood, David H. 1976. *Philosophies of Essence: An Examination of the Category of Essence.* Amsterdam: B. R. Gruner Publishing Company.

De Lauretis, Teresa. 1984. *Alice Doesn't: Feminism, Semiotics, Cinema.* Bloomington: Indiana University Press.

De Lauretis, Teresa (ed). 1986. *Feminist Studies/Critical Studies.* Bloomington: Indiana University Press.

De Lauretis, Teresa. 1987. *The Technologies of Gender: Essays on Theory, Film, and Fiction.* Bloomington: Indiana University Press.

Delphy, Christine. 1984. *Close to Home: A Materialist Analysis of Women's Oppression.* Trans. Diana Leonard. Amherst: University of Massachusetts Press.

De Man, Paul. 1984. *The Rhetoric of Romanticism*. New York: Columbia University Press.

D'Emilio, John. 1983. *Sexual Politics, Sexual Communities: The Making of a Homosexual Minority in the United States, 1940–1970*. Chicago and London: University of Chicago Press.

Derrida, Jacques. 1962. Translation and Introduction to Edmund Husserl, *L'Origine de la géométrie*. Paris: Presses Universitaires de France. Trans. John Leavey (1978). *Edmund Husserl's 'Origin of Geometry': An Introduction*. Pittsburgh: Duquesne University Press.

Derrida, Jacques. 1967a. *De la grammatologie*. Paris: Minuit. Trans. Gayatri Spivak (1976). *Of Grammatology*. Baltimore: Johns Hopkins University Press.

Derrida, Jacques. 1967b. *La voix et le phénomène: Introduction au problème du signe dans la phénomenologie de Husserl*. Paris: Presses Universitaires de France. Trans. David Allison (1973). *Speech and Phenomena: And Other Essays on Husserl's Theory of Signs*. Evanston: Northwestern University Press.

Derrida, Jacques. 1967c. *L'Ecriture et la différence*. Paris: Seuil. Trans. Alan Bass (1978). *Writing and Difference*. Chicago: University of Chicago Press.

Derrida, Jacques. 1972a. *La Dissémination*. Paris: Seuil. Trans. Barbara Johnson (1981). *Dissemination*. Chicago: University of Chicago Press.

Derrida, Jacques, 1972b. *Marges de la philosophie*. Paris: Minuit. Trans. Alan Bass (1982). *Margins of Philosophy*. Chicago: University of Chicago Press.

Derrida, Jacques. 1972c. *Positions*. Paris: Minuit. Trans. Alan Bass (1981). *Positions*. Chicago: University of Chicago Press.

Derrida, Jacques. 1974. *Glas*. Paris: Galilée. Trans. John P. Leavey and Richard Rand (1987). *Glas*. Lincoln: University of Nebraska Press.

Derrida, Jacques. 1977. "Fors." Trans. Barbara Johnson. *The Georgia Review* (Spring): 64–116.

Derrida, Jacques. 1978. *Éperons: Les styles de Nietzsche*. Paris: Flammarion. Trans. Barbara Harlow. 1979. *Spurs: Nietzsche's Styles*. Chicago: University of Chicago Press.

Derrida, Jacques. 1979a. "Living On: Borderlines." Trans. James Hulbert. *Deconstruction and Criticism*. New York: Seabury Press.

Derrida, Jacques. 1979b. "Me—Psychoanalysis: An Introduction to 'The Shell and the Kernel' by Nicolas Abraham." Trans. Richard Klein. *Diacritics* (Spring).

Derrida, Jacques. 1980. *La carte postale*. Trans. Alan Bass (1987). *The Post Card*. Chicago: University of Chicago Press.

Derrida, Jacques. 1982a. "Choreographies." Interview with Christie V. McDonald. *Diacritics* 12:2 (Summer): 66–76.

Derrida, Jacques. 1982b. *L'oreille de l'autre*. Trans. Peggy Kamuf (1985). *The Ear of the Other*. New York: Schocken Books.

Derrida, Jacques. 1984. "Women in the Beehive: A Seminar with Jacques Derrida." *subjects/objects* (Spring 1984). Reprinted in Jardine and Smith, 189–203.

Derrida, Jacques. 1985a. "Le Dernier Mot du Racisme." Trans. Peggy Kamuf. "Racism's Last Word." *Critical Inquiry* 12:1 (Autumn): 290–99.

Derrida, Jacques. 1985b. "Deconstruction in America: An Interview with Jacques Derrida." *Critical Exchange* 17 (Winter): 1–33.

Derrida, Jacques. 1986. "But, beyond . . . (Open Letter to Anne McClintock and Rob Nixon)." Trans. Peggy Kamuf. *Critical Inquiry* 13:1 (Autumn): 140–54.

Doane, Mary Ann. 1981. "Woman's Stake: Filming the Female Body." *October* 17: 23–36.

Doane, Mary Ann, Patricia Mellencamp and Linda Williams (eds). 1984. *Re-vision: Essays in Feminist Film Criticism*. Frederick, Md: University Publications of America and the American Film Institute.

Doane, Mary Ann. 1987. *The Desire to Desire*. Bloomington and Indianapolis: Indiana University Press.

Dollimore, Jonathan. 1986. "Homophobia and Sexual Difference." *Oxford Literary Review* 8:1–2: 5–12.

Du Bois, W.E.B. 1903. *The Souls of Black Folk*. In *Three Negro Classics*. New York: Avon Books, 1965.

Elshstain, Jean Bethke. 1983. "Homosexual Politics: The Paradox of Gay Liberation." In Boyers and Steiner, 252–80.

Epstein, Steven. 1987. "Gay Politics, Ethnic Identity: The Limits of Social Constructionism." *Socialist Review* 17:3/4 (May/August): 9–54.

Fanon, Frantz. 1952. *Peau Noire, Masques Blancs*. Paris: Editions de Seuil. Trans. Charles Lam Markmann (1967). *Black Skin, White Masks*. New York: Grove Press.

Faraday, Annabel. 1981. "Liberating Lesbian Research." In Plummer, 112–29.

Fauré, Christine. 1981. "The Twilight of the Goddesses, or the Intellectual Crisis of French Feminism." *Signs* 7:1 (Autumn): 81–6.

Féral, Josette. 1981. "Towards a Theory of Displacement." *Substance* 32: 52–64.

Ferguson, Ann. 1981. "Patriarchy, Identity, and the Sexual Revolution." *Signs* 7:1 (Autumn): 159–72.

Foucault, Michel. 1972. *The Archaeology of Knowledge and The Discourse on Language*. Trans. A. M. Sheridan Smith. New York: Pantheon Books.

Foucault, Michel. 1978. *The History of Sexuality, Volume I: An Introduction*. Trans. Robert Hurley. New York: Vintage.

Foucault, Michel. 1984. *The Foucault Reader*. Paul Rabinow (ed). New York: Pantheon.

Freud, Sigmund. 1920. "Psychogenesis of a Case of Homosexuality in a Woman." Vol. 18 of *The Standard Edition*. Trans. James Strachey. London: The Hogarth Press, 145–72.

Gallagher, Bob and Alexander Wilson. 1987. "Sex and the Politics of Identity: An Interview with Michel Foucault." In Mark Thompson (ed). *Gay Spirit: Myth and Meaning*. New York: St. Martin's Press.

Gallop, Jane. 1981. "Phallus/Penis: Same Difference." In Janet Todd (ed). *Men by Women*. Vol. 2 of *Women and Literature*. New York and London: Holmes & Meier, 243–51.

Gallop, Jane. 1982a. *The Daughter's Seduction: Feminism and Psychoanalysis*. Ithaca: Cornell University Press.

Gallop, Jane. 1982b. *"Writing and Sexual Difference:* The Difference Within." *Critical Inquiry* (Summer).

Gallop, Jane. 1983. "Quand nos lèvres s'écrivent: Irigaray's Body Politic." *Romanic Review* 74:1 (January): 77–83.

Gallop, Jane. 1985. *Reading Lacan.* Ithaca and London: Cornell University Press.

Gates, Henry Louis, Jr. (ed). 1984. *Black Literature & Literary Theory.* New York and London: Methuen.

Gates, Henry Louis, Jr. 1985. "Writing 'Race' and the Difference It Makes." *Critical Inquiry* 12:1 (Autumn): 1–20.

Gates, Henry Louis, Jr. (ed). 1986a. *"Race," Writing, and Difference.* Chicago: University of Chicago Press.

Gates, Henry Louis, Jr. 1986b. "Talkin' That Talk." *Critical Inquiry* 13:1 (Autumn): 203–10.

Gates, Henry Louis, Jr. 1987a. *Figures in Black: Words, Signs, and the "Racial" Self.* Oxford: Oxford University Press.

Gates, Henry Louis, Jr. 1987b. " 'What's Love Got To Do With It?' Critical Theory, Integrity, and the Black Idiom." *New Literary History* 18:2 (Winter): 345–62.

Gates, Henry Louis, Jr. 1988. *The Signifying Monkey.* Oxford: Oxford University Press.

Gentile, Mary. 1985. *Film Feminisms: Theory and Practice.* Westport, CN: Greenwood Press.

Gledhill, Christine. 1984. "Developments in Feminist Film Criticism." In Doane et al., 18–48.

Grahn, Judy. 1978. *The Work of a Common Woman.* New York: St. Martin's Press.

Greene, Gayle and Coppélia Kahn (eds). 1985. *Making a Difference: Feminist Literary Criticism.* London and New York: Methuen.

Griffiths, Morwenna and Margaret Whitford. 1988. *Feminist Perspectives in Philosophy.* Bloomington and Indianapolis: Indiana University Press.

Grimshaw, Jean. 1986. *Philosophy and Feminist Thinking.* Minneapolis: University of Minnesota Press.

Guha, Ranajit (ed). 1984. Vol. 3 of *Subaltern Studies: Writings on South Asian History and Society.* Delhi: Oxford University Press.

Halperin, David. 1986. "One Hundred Years of Homosexuality." *Diacritics* 16:2 (Summer): 34–45.

Hammond, Karla. 1980. "An Interview with Audre Lorde." *The American Poetry Review* (March/April): 18–21.

Haraway, Donna. 1985. "A Manifesto for Cyborgs: Science, Technology, and Socialist Feminism in the 1980's." *Socialist Review* 15:2 (March-April): 64–107.

Harris, Norman. 1987. " 'Who's Zoomin' Who': The New Black Formalism." *The Journal of the Midwest Modern Language Association* 20:1 (September): 37–45.

Hartman, Geoffrey. 1980. *Criticism in the Wilderness.* New Haven and London: Yale University Press.

Harvey, Irene E. 1986. *Derrida and the Economy of Différance.* Bloomington: Indiana University Press.

Heath, Stephen. 1978. "Difference." *Screen* 19:3 (Autumn): 50–112.

Heidegger, Martin. 1957. *Identity and Difference.* Trans. Joan Stambaugh (1969). New York: Harper & Row.

Hindess, Barry and Paul Hirst. 1975. *Pre-capitalist Modes of Production.* London and Boston: Routledge & Kegan Paul.

Hogue, W. Lawrence. 1985. "History, the Feminist Discourse, and Alice Walker's *The Third Life of Grange Copeland.*" *MELUS* 12:2 (Summer): 45–62.

Hogue, W. Lawrence. 1986. "Literary Production: A Silence in Afro-American Critical Practice." In Weixlmann and Fontenot, 31–45.

Husserl, Edmund. 1901. *Logical Investigations.* Vol. 2. Trans. J. N. Findlay. London: Routledge & Kegan Paul, 1970.

Huyssen, Andreas. 1984. "Mapping the Postmodern." *New German Critique* 33 (Fall): 5–52.

Irigaray, Luce. 1974. *Speculum de l'autre femme.* Trans. Gillian C. Gill (1985). *Speculum of the Other Woman.* Ithaca: Cornell University Press.

Irigaray, Luce. 1977a. *Ce Sexe qui n'en est pas un.* Trans. Catherine Porter with Carolyn Burke (1985). *This Sex Which Is Not One.* Ithaca: Cornell University Press.

Irigaray, Luce. 1977b. "Women's Exile." *Ideology and Consciousness* 1 (May): 62–76.

Irigaray, Luce. 1985. "Is the Subject of Science Sexed?" *Cultural Critique* 1 (Fall): 73–88.

Jacobus, Mary. 1982. "The Question of Language: Men of Maxims and *The Mill on the Floss.*" In Abel, 37–52.

Jakobson, Roman and Morris Halle. 1956. *Fundamentals of Language.* The Hague: Mouton Press.

Jameson, Fredric. 1982. Interview. *Diacritics* 12:3 (Fall 1982): 72–91.

Jardine, Alice. 1985. *Gynesis: Configurations of Woman and Modernity.* Ithaca and London: Cornell University Press.

Jardine, Alice and Paul Smith (eds). 1987. *Men in Feminism.* New York and London: Methuen.

Johnson, Barbara. 1980. *The Critical Difference: Essays in the Contemporary Rhetoric of Reading.* Baltimore and London: Johns Hopkins University Press.

Johnson, Barbara. 1984. "Metaphor, Metonymy and Voice in *Their Eyes Were Watching God.*" In Gates 1984, 205–219.

Jones, Ann Rosalind. 1985. "Inscribing Femininity: French Theories of the Feminine." In Greene and Kahn, 80–112.

Joyce, Joyce A. 1987a. "The Black Canon: Reconstructing Black American Literary Criticism." *New Literary History* 18:2 (Winter): 335–44.

Joyce, Joyce A. 1987b. " 'Who the Cap Fit': Unconsciousness and Unconscionableness in the Criticism of Houston A. Baker, Jr. and Henry Louis Gates, Jr." *New Literary History* 18:2 (Winter): 371–84.

Kamuf, Peggy. 1980. "Writing Like a Woman." In McConnell-Ginet et al., 284–99.

Kamuf, Peggy. 1982. "Replacing Feminist Criticism." *Diacritics* 12 (Summer): 42–47.

Kaplan, E. Ann. 1987. "Feminist Criticism and Television." In Robert C. Allen (ed). *Channels of Discourse: Television and Contemporary Criticism*. Chapel Hill and London: University of North Carolina Press.

Katz, Jonathan. 1976. *Gay American History: Lesbians and Gay Men in the U.S.A.* New York: Thomas & Cromwell Co., Inc.

Kinsman, Gary. 1987. *The Regulation of Desire: Sexuality in Canada*. New York and Montreal: Black Rose Books.

Koedt, Anne, Ellen Levine, and Anita Rapone (eds). 1973. *Radical Feminism*. New York: Quadrangle Books.

Kristeva, Julia. 1987. *The Kristeva Reader*. Toril Moi (ed). New York: Columbia University Press.

Lacan, Jacques. 1977. *Écrits*. Trans. Alan Sheridan. New York: W. W. Norton & Company.

Leitch, Vincent. 1983. *Deconstructive Criticism: An Advanced Introduction*. New York: Columbia University Press.

Lesselier, Claudie. 1987. "Social Categorizations and Construction of a Lesbian Subject." *Feminist Issues* (Spring): 89–94.

Locke, John. 1690. *An Essay Concerning Human Understanding*. London: Printed by Elizabeth Holt for Thomas Bassett.

MacCannell, Juliet Flower. 1986. *Figuring Lacan: Criticism and the Cultural Unconscious*. Lincoln: University of Nebraska Press.

Marks, Elaine. 1978. "Women and Literature in France." *Signs* 3:4 (Summer): 832–42.

Marks, Elaine. 1984. "Feminism's Wake." *Boundary 2* 12:2 (Winter): 99–110.

Martin, Biddy. 1982. "Feminism, Criticism, and Foucault." *New German Critique* 27 (Fall): 3–30.

McClintock, Anne and Rob Nixon. 1986. "No Names Apart: The Separation of Word and History in Derrida's 'Le Dernier Mot du Racisme.' " *Critical Inquiry* 13:1 (Autumn): 140–54.

McConnell-Ginet, Sally, Ruth Borker, and Nelly Furman (eds). 1980. *Women and Language in Literature and Society*. New York: Praeger.

McIntosh, Mary. 1968. "The Homosexual Role." *Social Problems* 16:2: 182–92.

McKeon, Richard (ed). 1941. *The Basic Works of Aristotle*. New York: Random House.

Merck, Mandy. 1987. "Difference and Its Discontents." *Screen* 28:1 (Winter): 2–9.

Miller, Nancy K. 1980. "Women's Autobiography in France: For a Dialectics of Identification." In McConnell-Ginet et al., 258–73.

Miller, Nancy K. 1982. "The Text's Heroine: A Feminist Critic and Her Fictions." *Diacritics* 12 (Summer): 48–53.

Miller, Nancy K. 1986a. "Changing the Subject: Authorship, Writing and the Reader." In de Lauretis, 102–120.

Miller, Nancy K. (ed). 1986b. *The Poetics of Gender*. New York: Columbia University Press.

Miller, R. Baxter. 1987. "Baptized Infidel: Play and Critical Legacy." *Black American Literature Forum* 21:4 (Winter): 393–413.

Minson, Jeff. 1981. "The Assertion of Homosexuality." *m/f* 5/6: 19–39.

Mitchell, Juliet and Jacqueline Rose. 1982. *Feminine Sexuality: Jacques Lacan and the école freudienne.* New York: W. W. Norton and Company.

Modleski, Tania. 1986. "Feminism and the Power of Interpretation: Some Critical Readings." In de Lauretis, 121–38.

Moi, Toril. 1985. *Sexual/Textual Politics: Feminist Literary Theory.* New York: Methuen.

Moraga, Cherríe. 1983. *Loving in the War Years.* Boston: South End Press.

Munitz, Milton K. 1971. *Identity and Individuation.* New York: New York University Press.

Omi, Michael and Howard Winant. 1986. *Racial Formation in the United States.* New York and London: Routledge & Kegan Paul.

Penley, Constance. 1986. "Teaching in Your Sleep." In Cary Nelson (ed). *Theory in the Classroom.* Urbana and Chicago: University of Illinois Press, 129–48.

Petersen, William. 1980. "Concepts of Ethnicity." In Stephen Thernstrom (ed). *Harvard Encyclopedia of American Ethnic Groups.* Cambridge, Mass: The Belknap Press, 234–42.

Plaza, Monique. 1978. " 'Phallomorphic Power' and the Psychology of 'Woman.' " *Ideology and Consciousness* 4 (Autumn): 57–76. Originally published in *Questions féministes* 1 (1978).

Plaza, Monique. 1981. "Our Damages and Their Compensation: Rape: The Will Not to Know of Michel Foucault." *Feminist Issues* (Summer): 25–35.

Plummer, Kenneth (ed). 1981. *The Making of the Modern Homosexual.* London: Hutchinson.

Radicalesbians. 1973. "The Woman Identified Woman." In Koedt et al., 240–45.

Ragland-Sullivan, Ellie. 1986. *Jacques Lacan and the Philosophy of Psychoanalysis.* Urbana and Chicago: University of Illinois Press.

Rich, Adrienne. 1983. "Compulsory Heterosexuality and Lesbian Existence." In Ann Snitow, Christine Stansell, and Sharon Thompson (eds). *Powers of Desire.* New York: Monthly Review Press, 177–205.

Rich, Adrienne. 1986. *Blood, Bread, and Poetry: Selected Prose 1979–1985.* New York and London: W. W. Norton & Company.

Riley, Denise. 1984. *War in the Nursery: Theories of the Child and the Mother.* London: Virago Books.

Robbins, Bruce. 1987/88. "The Politics of Theory." *Social Text* 18 (Winter): 3–18.

Rorty, Richard. 1979. *Philosophy and the Mirror of Nature.* Princeton: Princeton University Press.

Rose, Jacqueline. 1986. *Sexuality in the Field of Vision.* London: Verso.

Ruthven, K. K. 1984. *Feminist Literary Studies: An Introduction.* Cambridge: Cambridge University Press.

Said, Edward. 1986. "Intellectuals in the Post-Colonial World." *Salmagundi* 70–71 (Spring-Summer): 44–81.

Saussure, Ferdinand de. 1915. *Course in General Linguistics*. Trans. Wade Baskin (1959). New York: Philosophical Library.

Scholes, Robert. 1985. *Textual Power: Literary Theory and the Teaching of English*. New Haven and London: Yale University Press.

Scholes, Robert. 1987. "Reading Like a Man." In Jardine and Smith, 204–18.

Schor, Naomi. 1986a. "Introducing Feminism." *Paragraph* 8. Oxford University Press: 94–101.

Schor, Naomi. 1986b. "Reading Double: Sand's Difference." In Nancy K. Miller, 248–69.

Schor, Naomi. 1987. "Dreaming Dissymmetry: Barthes, Foucault, and Sexual Difference." In Jardine and Smith, 98–110.

Schor, Naomi. 1989. "This Essentialism Which is Not One: Coming to Grips With Irigaray." *Differences* 1:2 (Summer 1989).

Sedgwick, Eve Kosofsky. 1985. *Between Men: English Literature and Male Homosocial Desire*. New York: Columbia University Press.

Showalter, Elaine. 1982. "Feminist Criticism in the Wilderness." In Abel, 9–36.

Showalter, Elaine (ed). 1985. *The New Feminist Criticism: Essays on Women, Literature, and Theory*. New York: Pantheon Books.

Smith, Paul. 1988. *Discerning the Subject*. Minneapolis: University of Minnesota Press.

Spillers, Hortense J. 1987. "Mama's Baby, Papa's Maybe: An American Grammar Book." *Diacritics* (Summer): 65–81.

Spivak, Gayatri Chakravorty. 1983. "Displacement and the Discourse of Woman." In Mark Krupnick, (ed). *Displacement: Derrida and After*. Bloomington: Indiana University Press, 169–95.

Spivak, Gayatri Chakravorty. 1984. "Love Me, Love My Ombre, Elle." *Diacritics* (Winter): 19–36.

Spivak, Gayatri Chakravorty. 1986. "Imperialism and Sexual Difference." *Oxford Literary Review* 8:1–2, 225–40.

Spivak, Gayatri Chakravorty. 1987. *In Other Worlds: Essays in Cultural Politics*. New York and London: Methuen.

Stimpson, Catharine R. 1982. "Zero Degree Deviancy: The Lesbian Novel in English." In Abel, 243–59.

Tracy, Stephen. 1985. Review of Houston Baker's *Blues, Ideology, and Afro-American Literature*. *MELUS* 12:2 (Summer): 97–102.

Walker, Alice. 1983. *In Search of Our Mothers' Gardens*. New York: Harcourt Brace Jovanovich.

Ward, Jerry W. 1980. "The Black Critic as Reader." *Black American Literature Forum* 14:1 (1980): 21–23.

Washington, Booker T. 1901. *Up From Slavery*. In *Three Negro Classics*. New York: Avon Books, 1965.

Watney, Simon. 1980. "The Ideology of *GLF.*" In Gay Left Collective (eds). *Homosexuality: Power & Politics*. London and New York: Allison and Busby.

Watney, Simon. 1987. *Policing Desire: Pornography, AIDS and the Media.* Minneapolis: University of Minnesota Press.

Weeks, Jeffrey. 1977. *Coming Out: Homosexual Politics in Britain from the Nineteenth Century to the Present.* London: Quartet.

Weeks, Jeffrey. 1979. "Movements of Affirmation: Sexual Meanings and Homosexual Identities." *Radical History Review* 20 (Spring/Summer): 164–79.

Weeks, Jeffrey. 1985. *Sexuality and Its Discontents.* London: Routledge & Kegan Paul.

Weeks, Jeffrey. 1986. *Sexuality.* London and New York: Tavistock.

Weixlmann, Joe. 1986. "Black Literary Criticism at the Junctures." *Contemporary Literature* 27:1 (Spring): 48–62.

Weixlmann, Joe and Chester J. Fontenot (eds). 1986. *Studies in Black American Literature II.* Greenwood, Fla: The Penkevill Publishing Company.

Werner, Craig. 1986. "New Democratic Vistas: Toward a Pluralistic Geneology." In Weixlmann and Fontenot, 47–83.

Whitford, Margaret. 1986. "Luce Irigaray and the Female Imaginary: Speaking as a Woman." *Radical Philosophy* 43 (Summer): 3–8.

Wittig, Monique. 1979. "Paradigm." In Stambolian, George and Elaine Marks (eds). *Homosexualities and French Literature: Cultural Contexts/Critical Texts.* Ithaca: Cornell University Press, 114–21.

Wittig, Monique. 1980. "The Straight Mind." *Feminist Issues* (Summer): 103–111.

Wittig, Monique. 1981. "One is Not Born a Woman." *Feminist Issues* (Fall): 47–54.

Wittig, Monique. 1982. "The Category of Sex." *Feminist Issues* (Fall): 63–68.

Wittig, Monique. 1983. "The Point of View: Universal or Particular?" *Feminist Issues* (Fall): 63–69.

Wittig, Monique. 1986. "The Mark of Gender." In Nancy K. Miller, 63–73.

Zimmerman, Bonnie. 1985. "What Has Never Been: An Overview of Lesbian Feminist Literary Criticism." In Showalter, 200–24.

Index